The Theology of Rev. Twinkle Marie Manning

Living Life as a Prayer

The Theology of
Rev. "Twinkle" Marie Porter-Manning

Matrika Press
Rockwood, Maine

Living Life as a Prayer

The Theology of the
Rev. "Michelle" Marie Porter-Manning

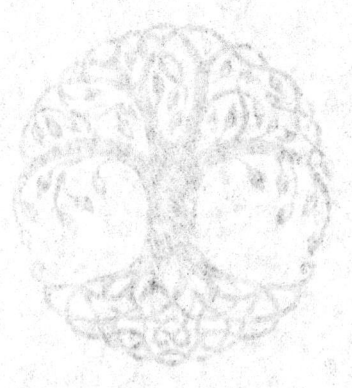

Manola Press
Rockwood, Maine

LIVING LIFE AS A PRAYER

THE THEOLOGY OF
Rev. "Twinkle" Marie Porter-Manning

Matrika Press
Rockwood, Maine

Copyright © Marie Porter-Manning
December 2020 hardcover
October 2020 paperback

All Rights Reserved
including the right of reproduction,
copying, or storage in any form
or means, including electronic,
In Whole or Part,
without prior written permission of the author.

Unless otherwise noted, poetry, blessings, meditations and prayers are written by Marie Porter-Manning. Additional credits in Cited Works portion.

ISBN: 978-1-946088-50-5
Library of Congress Control Number: 2020951474
Paperback ISBN: 978-1-946088-25-3; LCCN 2020949688

1.Religion 2.Spirituality 3.Transformation 4.Self-Exploration 5.Philosophy 5.Meditation 6.Creativity 7.Title

This book is for educational purposes.

Matrika Press

Matrika Press
P.O. Box 115
Rockwood, Maine 04478

Editor@MatrikaPress.com
www.MatrikaPress.com

First Edition Hardcover

This book contains the founding teachings of
The Church of Kineo
and Rev."Twinkle" Marie Porter-Manning's
seminal theology of *Living Life as a Prayer*.

To all who may be seeking a source of
spiritual renewal, may this book serve as a
guide for how to live a meaningful life.

"Magic exists. Who can doubt it, when there are rainbows and wildflowers, the music of the wind and the silence of the stars?"

Nora Roberts

"Each of us contains something within us which is unknown, but which, when it surfaces, is capable of producing miracles."

Paulo Coelho

Dedication

To Cindy Goldberg Newman.

Whenever I encounter moments of self-doubt, the cherished voice of your wisdom is recalled and ushers me to embrace life with clarity.

You blessed me with your honesty, your witness, your compassion, and your grace. I am ever grateful.

May you be blessed for you most assuredly are a blessing to the world!

Table of Contents

Preface	15
About Prayer	16
Introduction to Living Life as a Prayer	19
Review of Literature and Summary of Discernments	27
Discernments	39
Holy Ground	40
The Beloved Community, Anam Ċara & the Divine Echo	43
Möbius Living	57
Milestones, Thresholds & Rituals	71
In Our Own Image	76
Amalek Within	90
Love Enough	101
Undoubted Love: A Matter of Trust	117
Sacred Sexuality	123
Love Humanity's Children With Your Whole Heart	130
Borrowed Time	138
Death Changes Everything	144

Restore Us to Memory	154
Hospitality – a Pillar of Faith	168
Coming Home	171
Gentle Ripples	180
On Art and Centering	190
Sacred Service	196
Prelude to Be Like the Trees	205
Be Like the Trees	207
Of Awe and Grace	220
Weaving Harmony from Within the Chaos	230
Awakening Wisdom to Sabbatical Living	236
Love the Land You're With	244
Offerings and Stewardship	252
Open Hands - Living Life as a Prayer	254
Summary	264
Works Cited	272
Acknowledgements	280
Holy Days	282
Reflections	

PREFACE

The concepts in this book are the personal credo and theology of Rev. Dr. "Twinkle" Marie Porter-Manning. Much of the content was originally developed under the title *"Möbius Living as the Way of Building the Beloved Community and Healing the Loneliness that Exists in the World,"* for Rev. Manning's Doctor of Divinity dissertation. Her doctoral degree was awarded by the Department of Graduate Studies of the University of Sedona in November of 2017. Materials continued to be added to this content over an additional three year period under the overarching theme and title of *"Living Life as a Prayer."* This theology is the guiding work, principles and doctrines for *The Church of Kineo*, and shall continue to be expanded upon as a living tradition for people ever in discernment.

This book is presented for educational purposes to explore this theology. Inserted at the back is a partial list of *The Church of Kineo*'s *"Holy Days."*

~ Matrika Press, October 1st, 2020

ABOUT PRAYER

1-How do You pray? 2-How in your mind does prayer work?

Prayer to me is an active expression of my faith, a curiosity and a desire. The way I approach prayer has been informed by universal understandings, as well as personal experience.

Gregg Braden's book *Secrets of the Lost Mode of Prayer* really resonated with me a few years ago in the visualization aspects and conceptual embodiment of prayer. Likewise, the philosophy of Laura Day in *The Circle* where she effectively demonstrates how the power of a single wish can transform one's life.

To intend. To wish. To visualize. To embody.
To pray.

As a theist, prayer for me means intentionally connecting with and experiencing that which I call Holy. Daily I do so in stillness and silence, extending deep gratitude for Life and the gifts therein. Also, as a meditation practice, through reciting the druid-taught Aramaic version of the *Kabbalistic Cross* aloud as the vibration of the mantra brings me into full presence with the divinity in me and around me.

I turn to prayer in gratitude and also in surrender when circumstances are beyond my control. Sometimes my prayers manifest in writings and visualizations; oftentimes the simple act of touching my hand to my heart and humming (kind of like the Om) places me in conscious union with the divine.

There is holiness in quiet and in sound, in stillness and in movement.

I believe that prayer can be as diverse as that which we call Holy and can be made manifest through words, thoughts and deeds, such as daily acts of grace and gratitude.

I believe the energy of prayer can heal.

My theology is to Live Life as a Prayer

~ *Marie Porter-Manning*

INTRODUCTION TO LIVING LIFE AS A PRAYER

My life's path has taken me through the doors of many organizations and denominations with whom I have collaborated with on peace-building initiatives, justice movements and faith-based services and rituals. I was the Midwife and co-leader for the Women's Covenant Circle in Concord, Massachusetts for many years and have translated those duties into a more full-time and diverse role in a retreat home manifested for my family and I in Maine five and a half years ago, and another retreat home two years ago on Moosehead Lake. I have also a long history of retreat planning and pulpit supply for what I viewed as transformational religious churches and groups for most of the two past decades.

As my calling has become more clear, my ministry became more established, and requests for pastoral care and guidance from parishioners in churches I frequently serve and from participants in retreats and workshops I lead. Of primary concern to many in the spiritual circles I serve, even those who have been on spiritually enlightening journeys for many years, are feelings of separation, and of loneliness. Even within the realm of those seen by others as Masters in their fields, there are feelings of missing pieces in their strivings towards awakened holistic philosophies.

In my role as Minister and Worship Leader, for both laity and clergy, I have cultivated and taught my metaphysically-inclined meditations and faith-based intuitive spiritual practices that draw upon esoteric and nature-based modalities.

My ministry has evolved greatly over the past many years since my ordination with the International Metaphysical Ministry as well as my affiliation with various denominations. This book serves to mark my answering the call of my growing ministry in a fuller and deeper way that will be accessible to many through the establishment of *The Church of Kineo* and the sharing of the principles of *Living Life as a Prayer*.

There are concurrent and foundational themes in these teachings of Living Life as a Prayer. The principles of Möbius Living and Sabbatical Lifestyles, as well as creating The Beloved Community and connecting intentionally with that which we identify as Holy.

My hope is that you will find within this book, and within the teachings of Living Life as a Prayer, keys, mystical and physical, to experiencing this Human life to its fullest potential, and (hopefully) living your Spiritual calling therein.

A significant part of the mantle of this call is that of

awakening the relationship of our Soul Families while on Earth, and the nurturing of Spiritual Truths while incarnate. Throughout this book I cite some influential spiritual leaders I have had the pleasure to meet at intersections along my journey. Each aligning with my theology of Living Life as a Prayer. Each, in their own way, reminding us about the need for conscious connection with the Divine, and loving connection with each other as essential to a happy and fulfilled human experience.

Dr. Paul Leon Masters in his article entitled *"Loneliness - Mystically Perceived,"* in the November 22, 2015 edition of Mystical Insights Newsletter, says,

"Loneliness, mystically understood then, is isolation from God and thus, from the Presence of God within others." *(Masters/Mystical Insights)*

This book, and the doctrines of *Living Life as a Prayer* will serve as a stepping stone on the journey towards healing such perceived isolation and loneliness.

Much of my spirituality is informed by music and poetry. As such, so as to bring greater light and deeper philosophical perspective, songs and poems are inserted and referenced throughout this book. When the lyrics or poems are by authors other than myself, I cite them at the end of each piece. I also place in-text citations with my name for my own poems, blessings, prayers and musings to maintain continuity and eliminate confusion, yet I place them in italics to distinguish from the words and works of others.

Storytelling also plays a significant role in my ministry, so this book houses a few that relay pertinent messages to the overall themes.

My faith calls me to capitalize words that feel alive to me, sentient. Such words as "Love" and "Life" for they exhibit criteria for living beings in the way they expand and grow and live and die, while at the same time are eternal. Both also call us on to higher experiences of ourselves and each other, just as other living creatures we interact with and have relationships with.

The "Discernments" portion of this book draws in large part from the "Discussion" portion of my original doctoral dissertation. It describes three stages of relating: personal, intimate relationships, and the larger community as they apply to the theme of *Möbius Living as the Way of Building The Beloved Community and Healing the Loneliness that Exists in the World* and the overarching theme of *Living Life as a Prayer*. There are sub-chapters within the Discernments portion that delineate substantively the content. Each one systematically demonstrating perspectives that pertain to the overarching and foundational themes of this book.

Following in-line with its dissertation origins, this book carries footnotes and an appendix for reference-based study.

"The Beloved Community" is a phrase that was made popular when used by Dr. Martin Luther King, Jr. and was first cited to be uttered by Josiah Royce early in the 20th Century. (*Royce*)

Royce was the founder of the *Fellowship of Reconciliation*, which since 1915 has been at the forefront of creating and implementing programs and educational projects centered on nonviolent alternatives to conflict, including creative solutions to domestic and international peace and justice, as well as rights of conscience. King, Jr. was also a member of the *Fellowship of Reconciliation* movement. In addition to being one of the early pioneers in America of metaphysics, Royce embraced and evangelized absolute idealism in such a unified manner so as to include that everything we experience in our lives, even things that seem to not have rhythm or meaning, are in fact connected in pivotal ways to the whole of the experience. Such holistic philosophy pointing to the encompassment of universal reality, the interconnectedness of all beings, and thus of all consciousness.

It is my belief that this universal reality and interconnectedness can be seen in the microcosm of the individual's human experience, and in the macrocosm of Life on Planet Earth as we know it. It is my understanding that we are participants and that the Universe's function does not require our belief, but it receives our cooperation whether we are ready to acknowledge that or not. More than this, I have come to understand from both observation and personal experience that when one listens to the Universe, the Universe listens back.

Does time echo forward?

Or does it echo back?

It seems to me the latter.

But is it possible to track?

Coincidences coincide continually.

Yet are they purposeful perpetually?

It seems to me quite possibly.

But is this reality?

I believe it is, indeed, reality. And that in the Listening is found intuitive answers.

"Möbius Life" and "Living Life as a Prayer" were the themes of sermons I gave first at the Unitarian Universalist Church in Sangerville, Maine. The "Möbius Life" sermon gave a glimpse of living life from the inside out. It explored in-depth how that which is inside of us continually flows outward and that which is outside us continually flows inward, and how we can mindfully, creatively and intentionally live in such a way so as to enhance our experiences and our lives. "Living Life as a Prayer" allows us to be active co-creators in our inner and outer worlds. Such a life is one of peaceableness and mindful authenticity.

Möbius Living by Living Life as a Prayer, contemplatively and practically, can create The Beloved Community as it reengages us with the ultimate Truth that we are all universally connected to each other and to Source, and, as such, motivates us to model unconditional welcome and radical hospitality. This book explores deeply into this theory and demonstrates how the universal and metaphysical philosophies applied can transform our human experiences and heal the loneliness that exists in our world.

Introduction to Living Life as a Prayer

While the majority of the theology in this book are teachings I have been preaching and sharing throughout my tenure as a minister, there is a certain poignancy to have the publishing of *Living Life as a Prayer* be occurring during a global pandemic. As I write this final note for the introduction, many around the globe remain Sheltered in Place, working from home, engaging in remote learning, and considering (some perhaps for the first time) what kind of "normal" we wish to create in our lives. The principles of Sabbatical Living and Weaving Harmony from Chaos are valuable insights and real possibilities for humanity.

May the ideals, philosophies and teachings of Living a Life as a Prayer resonate with you. And, if it does, please reach out to us at **The Church of Kineo**.

Sending Love and prayers of Blessed Be and Amen to all who are inspired by this book.

~ "Twinkle" Marie Porter-Manning,
September 27th, 2020

Review of Literature and Summary of Discernments

Within the content of this book (and the original dissertation), myriad books, novels, songs, poems, prayers, mediations, websites and other quotations are cited. The first quotation is from Dr. Paul Leon Masters, found in the November 22, 2015 edition of Mystical Insights Newsletter. I felt it important to draw from his insights in this paper, as he is the founder of the University of Sedona, and the International Metaphysical Ministries of which I am ordained. His weekly emails, even the ones we receive in memorandum, are a source of inspiration and reflection in a world where chaos often reigns. The quote I selected was one about loneliness and feelings of separateness as I believe these two things are symptoms that can be healed when we apply the teachings of Möbius Living as we build The Beloved Community.

The Discernments portion of this book holds sub-chapters, each containing wisdom from relevant sources. Below is a delineation of each chapter's related literature:

- ***"Holy Ground"*** highlights a beautiful chant by Linda Smith Koehler reminding us that we are always and ever in the presence of the Divine. In this chapter, Rev. Meg Riley is quoted for a stirring call to action she compels us towards co-creating the Holy on Earth.

- ***"The Beloved Community, Anam Ċara & the Divine Echo"*** is a rich chapter that identifies our Soul Family and asks us to pay attention to the inner-knowing we have that testifies to the Divinity in each other. At the outset of this chapter an *Ojibway Prayer* reminding us that healing can take place, when we reconnect with each other. In this chapter Rev. Ian White Maher my friend and colleague is introduced with his prolific teaching that, when you bless someone, everything in your life changes. Ian is an ordained minister and I was a member of his advisory group to help him shape a spiritual discernment program to help people looking to deepen their spiritual lives in order to engage more in the world around us, namely, for people who believe we need a transformation in our culture, a transformation grounded in a deeper spiritual appreciation of who we are. It is a mechanism of the discipleship of building The Beloved Community. This is in complete alignment with Irish Philosopher John O'Donohue tellings of the impact of our *Anam Ċara*: Soul Friends. Ralph Waldo Emerson, American essayist, lecturer, poet and Transcendentalist who lived in the 1800s, ardently speaks about what real friendships are. Whereas Aristotle is drawn from to bring more clarity about the highest kinds of friendships. *A Course in Miracles* writer, Helen Schucman, relays how each of us are mirrors to the other. And that when we offer up our light to our brothers and sisters, it is then that we recognize it as our own. Poet David Whyte speaks of the enduring tests of authentic friendships that can exist only when tolerance and mercy are ever-present, and the kind of community we need to make us stronger as we navigate our journeys. Author Anne Lamott's words are quoted from *Small Victories: Spotting Improbable Moments of Grace*, reminding us in allegory of practical lighthouses who stand there shining their light, beaconing in welcome that it is a source of safety.

- **"Möbius Living"** features songwriters Sara Dan Jones, Pat Humphries and Bob Dylan, and their respective songs, "Breathe in Peace," "Swimming to the Other Side," and "All Along the Watchtower." Each song offering a deeper understanding of the concept of the Möbius and embracing Möbius Living in our hearts and in our practices is a clear path towards creating The Beloved Community. Also featured in this chapter is Mitch Albom's story about the farmer's helper who was prepared to weather any storm in his book *"Have a Little Faith."*

- **"Milestones, Thresholds & Rituals"** speaks to ancient human inclinations toward ritual and highlights some of the locations throughout this book that contain relevant rituals and writings to honor the Holy Days in our lives - and touches upon why it is important to do so.

Living Life as a Prayer

- *"In Our Own Image"* offers an alternate perspective of how we envision the Holy. A poignant uncovering of David Foster Wallace's Commencement Speech: *"This is Water"* targets our created realities of gods we serve and how, depending on which we choose, will either eat us alive or bring us tremendous joy and connection to source and to each other. This chapter also cites from the New International Version (NIV) of The Holy Bible: the Book of Ecclesiastes and 1 Corinthians 13:11-14. Offering insights about love from both King Solomon and the Apostle Paul. Liberal religious ministers Rev. Marlin Lavanhar, Rev. David Ruffin, and Rev. Naomi King are each referenced from sermons they've given, that draw us closer towards trusting that the only god to believe in is a god of love, and that we are called to be instruments of love and practicers of transcendence. Quotes from *Metaphysically Speaking*, a book by Rev. Dr. Della Reese Lett, provide examples of affirmations we can use to connect with Source. Additionally, Fredrik Backman, author of A Man Called Ove and Jane Roberts whose works are recorded at The Seth Learning Center, both point to the innate power of intimate relationships. Poet Anne Bradstreet brings this idea of god in our own image full circle with her beseeching poem in *Contemplations* in recognition of the divinity of Nature.

- *"Amalek Within"* addresses the darker aspects of human-nature. This chapter reasons that individually and collectively we are influenced by internal and external forces. Here, we confront the fact we each carry with us both elation and heartbreak and it is up to us to create a space so sacred so as to encompass it all. This chapter gives insight on the ancient Amalekite tribe of Israel as referred to in the Hebrew Scriptures and as spoken of by Rabbi Daniel Bogard in a recent sermon. Teachings of Carlos Castaneda regarding prevailing dark forces as well as examples of historical "adversaries" are presented from a variety of religious and spiritual backgrounds, including Christian, Buddhist, Druid, Ojibwa, and Transcendental. Philosopher Ralph Waldo Emerson in his writings, Mystic Eckhart Tolle in his book entitled *Stillness Speaks* and Psychoanalyst Carl Jung's book *Psychology and Religion* are quoted in reference to that which we call Ego. This chapter also references Rev. Ian White Maher in his practical and ever spiritual advice to turn towards God in prayer; to invite God in to mentor and to heal what is before us. Examples of prayers are included as written by Rev. Dr. Della Reese Lett in her book, *Metaphysically Speaking*, as well as in the *Druidic Craft of the Wise: Student Handbook* published by the Grove of the Sacred Oak.

- ***"Love Enough"*** explores the idea that love is a gift to be given in love. Roman Krznari's 2013 article in *Yes! Magazine* entitled: *"The Ancient Greeks' 6 Words for Love (And Why Knowing Them Can Change Your Life)"* provides as a reference about various kinds of love. Texts quoted in this chapter include Thich Nhat Hanh's book *True Love: A Practice for Awakening the Heart* which points to the source of human suffering and the express definition of what True Love is, and what it is not. Erich Fromm's book *The Art of Loving* and Gary Chapman's *The Five Love Languages: How to Express Heartfelt Commitment to Your Mate* each provide insights about how we can best express love. Songs cited in this chapter include: Nat King Cole's *"Nature Boy"* and Antonio Carlos Jobim's *"Wave."* Each of these offering deeper insights on the true meanings and aspects of love and how best to live into loving practices. This theme is made complete with words from Lebanese-American Sufi, artist, poet, and writer Khalil Gibran.

- *"Undoubted Love: A Matter of Trust"* expands on discernments revealed in "Love Enough." This sub-chapter cites Dr. Brené Brown's *"Seven Elements of Trust"* found in her Super Soul Sessions talk, *The Anatomy of Trust*. This chapter affirms that Love is beautiful, and loving takes work.

- *"Sacred Sexuality"* features an excerpt from a sermon given by Rev. Laura Horton-Ludwig entitled, "Sexuality and Spirituality." Also, quotes from Starhawk's Beacon Press release: *"Dreaming the Dark: Magic, Sex and Politics"* and Thomas Moore's book, *"The Soul of Sex."* Each of these offering content to better shape our understandings as to why our culture has become estranged from our sexuality, and why it is vital we bring it back home to reside with us in its rightful place among all elements of our spirituality. Cited as well are three online magazines that report documented findings on the practical benefits of active sexuality: PsychologyToday, CBSNews.com, Women'sHealthMagazine, as well as Dr. Mercola's aggregated website.

- *"Love Humanity's Children with Your Whole Heart"* in no uncertain terms bequeaths to readers their responsibility for our present and future generations. The onus is on every single one of us to heal ourselves so that we can care for our children in ways they deserve. Also, pointedly, without mistake, we are directed as to how "not" to treat children. This chapter explores the importance of loving children. It first speaks frankly about the harm that is all too often done to children either in ignorance, unconsciousness, or willful disrespect of their agency. Then, moving on to how to create environments and family lifestyles where children can thrive it calls upon insights from world experts. Dr. Shefali Tsabary speaks to the ways we best empower our children during Oprah Winfrey's *Super Soul Sessions*. Sharifa Oppenheimer seminal work, *Heaven on Earth: a Handbook for Parents of Young Children*, maps out important aspects to include in the family culture and ways to create nourishing environments for children. Julia Cameron *The Artist's Way for Parents* offers insights about how to embrace and enhance our children's creativity.

- **"Borrowed Time"** reminds us how precious Time is, and that while we do not want to get distracted by the illusion of Time, we do want to be mindful of it. This theme is brought to light with the words of Mary Oliver in her poem *"The Summer Day"* and by henry David Thoreau's words from his book, *Walden*.

- **"Death Changes Everything"** touches upon various belief structures of the hereafter and afterlife. It brings to the fore the necessity of grief and grieving and moving forward when someone we love dies. Highlighted here are words of wisdom from Author Nora McInerny and Poet Dianalee Velie, who both speak to how joy exists amid grief. This chapter contains two of my most personal musings written during deep grief after the death of my 22 year old son in 2019.

- **"Restore Us to Memory"** brings us back to the Truth of who we are within ourselves and for each other. Essentially, that we are each others keepers (of memory) and how we can assure strength in our abilities of memory. We explore *"Brigid of the*

Mantle" a goddess chant from which we gain the them of, *"Restore us to memory,"* and a Cherokee/Navajo Proverb oft turned into a chanting hymn for meditation, *"When you were born,"* that impels us to live a life that we rejoice. John Coleman Darnell work with the *Elkab Desert Archaeological Survey Project* is cited. As it is worth repeating, the words from Linda Smith Koehler's "Holy Ground" are cited. Included in this chapter is also Sheryl Cr*ow's song,* "Love Will Remain" which reminds us of what is truly important.

- **"Hospitality – a Pillar of Faith"** draws upon ancient Irish wisdom, along with more words from Rev. Ian White Maher in his sermon entitled, *"Prophetic Evangelism."*

- **"Coming Home"** highlight's Starhawk's vision of a "Circle of Friends" as found in her book *Dreaming the Dark,* "The Winds of Summer" by Patricia Shuttee and the "Women's Water Ritual" created by Carolyn McDade and Lucile Schuck Longview.

- **"Gentle Ripples"** reminds us of the importance of bringing all that we are to our communities, our gifts and our burdens, our joys and our sorrows. This section lifts up the words and wisdom of: Buddhist teacher, Tara Brach regarding compassion; Rev. Stephen Shiek describing the sacred places we create and that are indeed waiting for us; and, Coretta Scott King who talks about the strength of community. *"Gentle Ripples"* includes an adaptation of the original Water Ritual, including a basketful of stones, the stones resembling the multitude of ways our sorrows and our burdens manifest in our lives, the ritual allowing us to let them go, or, alternately, sharing the burden with our community so we do not have to carry them alone.

The Theology of Rev. Twinkle Marie Manning

- **"On Art and Centering"** points the works and wisdom of M.C. Richards, Anne Morrow Lindbergh, and Lucy Maude Montgomery within their respective books, *Centering: in Pottery, Poetry, and the Person*; *Gift from the Sea*; and, *Anne of Green Gables*. Each of these iconic women show us the importance of staying true to our Life's callings even as we tune into the centrifugal force that is our connection to the universe. Also cited in this chapter are the words of my former pottery teacher, Carl Phyllis, a Canadian artist, whose thoughtfulness helped shape not only my pottery practice, but the ever expanding theme of the Möbius Life.

- **"Sacred Service"** offers clarity around the places where spirituality and activism can intersect in healthy ways as Spiritual Activism. While *The Church of Kineo* and *Living Life as a Prayer* has clear separation of "church" and "state," we recognize that members and individuals may feel called to social or spiritual activism as an outward manifestation of their specific beliefs. This section spotlights some renown modern day social-spiritual activists, such as Rev. Peter Morales who affirms that service is his religion's prayer; Seane Corn, who discusses waking up and discovering her purpose; and Mona Miller who succinctly defines spirituality as Truth and Love. As well included are ancient understandings about justice as found in the book of Isaiah.

- **"Be Like the Trees"** weaves together a collage of insights and inspirations directing towards the interconnectedness and magic of human existence. This section candidly looks at tragedy, grief, and challenges faced in daily life. Citing the works of Sarah Addison Allen in *First Frost*; Natalie Goldberg's *Writing*

Down the Bones; Julia Butterfly Hill's *The Legacy of Luna*; and Jane Roberts' poignant observations, each illustrating our interconnection and impact on each other. Also included are inspiring words from Saint Francis of Assisi and the Serenity Prayer. We learn how to face, enter, embrace, and go through The Afterward of life's tragedies and live in a way that emulates our knowing that we are all connected. And, citing Ecologist Suzanne Simard, we can discern that like a forest, humans too can have a symbiotic communication system that informs of danger, and assists when needed.

- **"Of Awe and Grace"** informs us that our human lives are made up of recognizable moments that render us in absolute awe of the miraculous we see before us. May Sarton's vision of *"Being," "immortality,"* and *"destiny"* are included as a prelude. We dive into the hidden deep and dormant meanings active in our language as explained by Rev. Cathie Stivers in *Reviving Our Indigenous Souls, How to Practice the Ancient to Bring in the New.* Rev. Stivers artfully guides readers through the embodied ancient memory encoded in our Etymology. We journey via story and myth citing moments in *The City of Angels* movie worth our consideration. Also cited is the Universal Law of Oneness, per Hereditary Chief, Phil Lane Jr. and Meister Eckhart's idea of the greatest prayer. We learn what truly defines a miracle according to Rev. Kate Braestrup in her book, *Here if You Need Me. Of Awe and Grace* encourages readers to hone the practice of *Living Life as a Prayer* in awe and in grace, and greet life's everyday miracles with reverence.

- **"Weaving Harmony from Within the Chaos"** is a unique merging of poetry, music and stream of consciousness. It provides courage and strength to face uncertain moments with intentionality, and, in doing so, revealing the unimaginable beauty that is often found to exist therein. Included are the two-part *"Kinship"* poem by Angela Morgan, the *"Breathing"* song meditation by Sarah Dan Jones, and insights of Sufi Mystic, Hazrat Inayat Khan.

- ***"Awakening Wisdom to Sabbatical Living"*** explores what a blessing a Sabbatical Lifestyle can be if it were included in everyone's *Wheel of the Year*, rather than merely being relegated for the tenured and the elite. Quoted works include: *Reviving Our Indigenous Souls, How to Practice the Ancient to Bring in the New* by Rev. Cathie Stivers, and *Bird by Bird, Some Instructions on Writing and Life* by Anne Lamott.

- ***"Offerings and Stewardship"*** explores the history of tithing in support of one's religious community. Tithing should not be a hardship on the giver, neither should it be a pittance. Gifts should be given from the heart, in recognition and gratitude for the spiritual nourishment one receives.

- ***"Open Hands - Living Life as a Prayer"*** is both a call to action, and its answer with John Lennon's *"Imagine"* setting the tone at the outset. When we *Live Life as a Prayer*, we draw close to and experience *The Holy Quiet* that is our sacred connection to Source and to each other. We recognize with clarity the callings of our heart; the Callings from God and we live our lives in answer to this call. Cited in this chapter are the words of James Martineau and Edwin Markham, liberal religious forefathers, who foreshadowed much of what is now spoken in the New Thought movement. Their poems, sermons and essays point to the kinds of practices we wish to model as we embody Möbius Living. Markham speaks of drawing a circle that draws others in. Martineau speaks of revealing our authenticity in the soliloquies of the unguarded mind. Living Life as a Prayer, we are open and accessible, so others can look into our hearts and see that which we revere. And, living life as a prayer, we heed the Golden Rule as given to us by Jesus in Matthew chapters 6 and 7 where he says, *"do to others what you would have them do to you."* (NIV)

In addition to the above cited literature, this book contains several of my original blessings, prayers and mediations placed throughout to further emphasize and exemplify the messages being brought forth. These are often placed with highlighted backgrounds.

Discernments

Living Life as a Prayer

HOLY GROUND

*"Where ever you are
you are on holy ground;
When ever you are
you are living in sacred time;
Who ever you are with
you are in the presence of the divine;
So keep that in mind,
Keep that in mind."*

(Smith Koehler 15)

This chant entitled "Holy Ground" found on page 15 in the songbook: *Women With Wings: Original Chants and Songs of Affirmation and Empowerment* published by Quiet Waters Publications in 2005 by Linda Smith Koehler, current leader of the Women With Wings singing group located in Bangor, Maine, aptly sums up the universal reality I believe we all have access to here on Earth. It also gives us reason to pause and reflect on the fact that every single moment we choose to remember this, acknowledge it, and act from a place of understanding, is a moment we choose to live in the sphere of personal accountability and creativity.

Remembering we are on Holy Ground infuses our desire to be good stewards of Earth. Acknowledging we are Living in Sacred Time provides us a spiritual framework and measuredly accessible space from which to work within. Keeping in mind that every single encounter we have with another, is that of being in the Presence of the Divine holds us accountable to the most treasured of Truths. That we are One. That we are meant to be our sister's and our brother's keepers. That our choices in how we treat each other matter. That the Divinity in each of us is kin to that in all others.

This place of grounding, this holy ground, this sacred time, this presence of the divine are each individually, and as a whole, foundational for us to understand should we wish to experience the fullness of life while in human form. And, most certainly, they are among the keys to creating The Beloved Community. With that in mind, I point to the words of Rev. Meg Riley, who charges us with this thought:

"To commit to creating

a prophetic congregation today

is to grapple with what it means

to take responsibility for co-creating

the holy right here on earth." *(Riley)*

Every time we gather together as a faith-based community we have the opportunity to co-create the holy together. We have all the elements needed: place, time and each other as divinity incarnate.

Seeking, and discovering, Heaven on Earth, can be as simple as opening the doors to our churches and offering authentic Welcome. Creating The Beloved Community is living in to that Welcome Together, prophetically, thoughtfully, from the inside out and the outside in.

The Theology of Rev. Twinkle Marie Manning

THE BELOVED COMMUNITY, ANAM CARA & THE DIVINE ECHO

Consider with me this: There is a divine echo that whispers within every heart. Indeed, that every soul carries with it the echo of a intrinsic intimacy. An original echo that is brought fourth through time from original source. A primal source where we are all One. Where intimacy has no limit and love has no barrier. And we carry the essence of this original echo as a talisman of our divinity and a reminder of the vast belonging we are capable of. Because it is who we are. We Belong to each other.

Consider that this divine echo, the one I carry, the ones carried by others, are in constant recognition of each other. When we are harmonious with each other, the recognition alights us with positive, light, joyful, peaceful feelings. Whereas, the negative, sad, fearful or angry emotions we feel about each other are a result of the echo noticing the disharmony with Oneness.

The Celtic Spiritual Tradition has a phrase that identifies this sense of Oneness. It is called Anam Ċara. Soul Friends. More than words, it is a concept imbued with deep meaning. Derived from the understanding of the Soul as a divine echo.

Consider that each of our Souls have a signature

resonance that radiates throughout and around our physical bodies. And that when we come in contact with others, especially our *Anam Ċara*, an awakening takes place. An awareness of the connection.

In our modern day, some romanticize this feeling and create limits around its capacity. Suggesting only one other person on this entire planet could be your *Anam Ċara*. A soul mate. Or sole mate. Singular. But the embodiment of *Anam Ċara* is much more far-reaching than that.

Anam Ċara is a blessing we all have access to and can share with each other. When you have found the most sacred place of belonging, where your inner light recognizes and is recognized by those in your company, you have found home.

When you have found the most sacred place of belonging, where your inner light recognizes and is recognized by those in your company, you have found home. This is The Beloved Community.

And it is there that *Anam Ċara* resides.
It is there that *Anam Ċara* can be explored.

It is also there that *Anam Ċara* can be challenged. And will be. For it is within our most intimate relationships that our deep bonds are formed. And to experience intimacy, one must be vulnerable. And to be vulnerable in the midst of others who are as imperfectly perfect as we are, we risk being hurt. But we also open to being nurtured and healed.

To understand the concept of Oneness and *Anam Ċara* from the aspect of The Beloved Community, we must explore what it means to Belong to one another.

What responsibilities come with this belonging? There is an Ojibway Prayer with numerous variations said to be originally written by Art Solomon, an Ojibway spiritual elder from Ontario, Canada, which speaks to such belonging. One version of this profound prayer reads:

"*Grandfather,*
Look at our brokenness.
We know that in all creation
Only the human family
Has strayed from the Sacred Way.
We know that we are the ones
Who are divided;
And we are the ones
Who must come back together
to worship and walk in the Sacred Way.
Grandfather,
Sacred One,
Teach us love, compassion, and honor.
Teach us how to heal our brokenness,
That we may heal the earth
And heal each other."
(Solomon)

When our faith compels us to recognize the light of divinity we each carry within us, each adding to the flame of love, we are motivated to find ways back to our connectedness when we wander to far from Center. We are stronger together. We are better together. We are meant to be together. It is our nature and our purpose to find our way back to each other, for it is in our togetherness that we heal and thrive.

Living Life as a Prayer

There is a childhood cliche that has turned into a story for all ages I share during services speaking about The Beloved Community:

> *I grew up in Canada and one of the common sayings we would hear from adults when we did something that was bizarre or made them laugh was, "Oh, you silly goose!"*
>
> *When I was considering which Children's Message to tell for our Time for All Ages during our service theme of Belonging to one another, I could not think of a better story than that of the geese.*
>
> *When we think of geese, we usually think of the aerodynamic way they fly. Their V-formation instantly recognizable as a flock of geese. We can imagine that they fly in that configuration to conserve energy, flying with more speed and ease, and protection from predators and elements.*
>
> *It is interesting to note that the goose leading the flock, is not always the same goose. They change positions, sharing the leadership, so that no one goose gets too tired.*
>
> *Also, should one goose get hurt, or shot, and fall to the ground, two additional geese drop out of the flock and go to the ground with the injured goose. And they remain with the injured goose until he is either ready to fly again and rejoin the flock, or he dies. Only then, do the two sentinel geese return to the flock. Geese – not so silly after all!*

In similar ways, a strong beloved community emulates the example of geese: sharing leadership and ministering to one another when members are in need. We help each other on our journeys because we belong to one another. As such it is essential that we foster deep relationships with those to whom we belong.

I ask you to consider that while we may know things about each other, it does not mean we *know* each other. Yes, while we may know things *about* each other, it does not mean we *know* each other. Opening to *Anam Ċara* gives us the opportunity to *know* each other. Anam Ċara. Soul Friends. Within The Beloved Community. Consider that *this Divine Echo* is our touchstone; our reminder that we are *Anam Ċara*. And our promise that we are blessings to each other.

Rev. Ian White Maher tells us that when you bless someone, everything in your life changes. Similarly, Irish Philosopher John O'Donohue in his *Friendship Blessing* found in *Anam Ċara: A Book of Celtic Wisdom* published in 1998, suggests that our *Anam Ċara* relationships have the power to, "transfigure that which is negative, distant or cold" and can create "the gentle nest of belonging" we all long for. (O'Donohue, 36)

Throughout time many have spoken about the priceless value of friendship, *and of friendship's complexities*. Liberal religious forefather, Ralph Waldo Emerson is known to have asserted:

"I do not wish to treat friendships daintily, but with roughest courage. When they are real, they are not glass threads or frost-work, but the solidest thing we know." *(Emerson)*

Aristotle spoke of the highest kind of friendship being one of virtue. The kind of friendship where you are friends with someone because of the kind of person he or she is; that is, because of his or her virtues. In Aristotle's day "virtues" would have meant ethics. Within the realm of *The Church of Kineo* faith tradition, we would be speaking of our shared values and how we live into them. Aristotle spoke too of the partnership of friendships, the idea of the virtuous friend as *"another self."* Joined as in the echo of divinity. Friends holding mirrors up to one another so they have access to see themselves, and each other, more fully. And in doing so, improve the quality of the people they are. And in doing that, enhance the quality of the friendships they share.

Helen Schucman in relaying *A Course in Miracles* also refers to the mirror of friendships. She says:

"Your (sibling) is the mirror in which you see the image of yourself." (VII:1)

She urges us to seek to recognize our brothers and sisters, our spiritual siblings, both as a means for salvation and as a mechanism of blessing and being blessed. She affirms:

"You will not see the light until you offer it to your brothers. As they take it from your hands, so will you recognize it as your own" (L153)

She declares that when we meet anyone to remember it is a holy encounter.

"As you see (your sibling) you will see yourself. As you treat (them) you will treat yourself. As you think of (them) you will think of yourself. Never forget this, for in (them) you will find yourself or lose yourself." (VIII:4)

She continues by explaining:

"Whenever two (Children) of God meet they are given another chance at salvation." (VIII:4)

She says:

"Do not leave anyone without giving salvation to (them) and receiving it yourself." (VIII:4)

In other words, your *Anam Ċara* is always there with you, in remembrance of you.

Poet and Author David Whyte in his literature and on his social media pages takes this theme to an even deeper level, in an excerpt on his Facebook page from his 2014 book *CONSOLATIONS: The Solace, Nourishment and Underlying Meaning of Everyday Words*, published by Many Rivers Press, suggesting:

Friendship is not only a mirror to presence but a testament to forgiveness.

He says:

"Friendship not only helps us see ourselves through another's eyes, but can be sustained over the years only with someone who has repeatedly forgiven us for our trespasses as we must find it in ourselves to forgive them in turn. A friend knows our difficulties and shadows and remains in sight, a companion to our vulnerabilities more than our triumphs, when we are under the strange illusion we do not need them. An undercurrent of real friendship is a blessing exactly because its elemental form is rediscovered again and again through understanding and mercy. All friendships of length are based on a continued, mutual forgiveness. Without tolerance and mercy all friendships die." (*Whyte*)

Whyte says:

"In the course of the years a close friendship will always reveal the shadow in the other as much as ourselves, to remain friends we must know the other and their difficulties and even their sins and encourage the best in them, not through critique but through addressing the better part of them, the leading creative edge of their incarnation, thus subtly discouraging what makes them smaller, less generous, less of themselves." (*Whyte*)

"And yet, friendship is a merited grace, one that requires of us the unrelenting commitment of being present with and bearing witness to one another, over and over." (*Whyte*)

It is within the sacred space of this deep dynamic of friendship that we not only know things about each other, but where we really know each other.

A Blessing of our Mirrors in Friendship

May we hold our mirrors lovingly in friendship
to allow us to fully understand ourselves
and each other.
May these mirrors reflect in kindness
what we most need to see.
May we understand that we are

> capable of being loved
> no matter what wounds we still carry,
> no matter what mistakes we still make.
> May we know that we are capable
> of loving generously,
> even beyond our wildest imaginations.
> May we see beyond the shadow
> and into the Soul.
>
> Amen and Blessed Be.

My friend and colleague, Ian White Maher, whose words I shared earlier in this portion of this book, revealing to us that when we bless someone everything in our life changes. He also talks about our deep need for Empathetic Witness. The kind of seeing, and being seen, that only happens in the close circles of family, of community, of relationships. That's right, in our *Anam Cara* friendships.

In the Buddhist tradition, this kind of friendship is called *"Kalyana-mitra"* meaning the "Noble Friend."

Kalyana-mitra/Noble Friends have no pretense between them. They witness in empathy and in action, with clear communication and by gentle strength confronting each other with our blind spots. Friendships at this level are able to navigate challenges and heal wounds for they are willing to negotiate beyond the awkwardness and uncertainties that are paramount when our vulnerabilities are exposed.

It requires humility as well to be open to seeing through another's eyes what we are unable to perceive on our own. It requires grace to *accept* this sight without defensiveness. It requires grace to *offer* this sight without judgement. To be present with each other in this way is a testament of trust and the embodiment of faith.

And faith is certainly needed when we shine the gentle light of the Soul on our wounds. We are indeed a wounded gift to each other, but a beloved gift nonetheless.

David Whyte speaks about the benefit of this depth of friendship in saying:

"The ultimate touchstone of friendship is witness, the privilege of having been seen by someone and the equal privilege of being granted the sight of the essence of another, to have walked with them and to have believed in them, and sometimes just to have accompanied them on a journey impossible to accomplish alone." (*Whyte*)

For some believe it is the hard times that make us stronger, yet I believe it is the **good** <u>we are wrapped up in</u> while facing hard times that help us carry our broken pieces: the love of our family, our friends, our community, these are what make us stronger, keep us whole, keep us moving forward. This **good** is the beloved community we all seek to belong to.

As a faith community, how do we become accessible to facilitating the nurturing of *that* kind of friendships? Author Anne Lamott has some advice for us in her legendary book, *Bird by Bird: Some Instructions on Writing and Life*, where we could see ourselves as a Lighthouse. She points out that:

"Lighthouses don't go running all over an island looking for boats to save; they just stand there, shining." (*Bird*, 31)

Every day that those of us called to ministries that actively create The Beloved Community in our churches and retreat centers, with doors open in welcome, we stand as a lighthouse, shining, beckoning those who would be saved into our loving embrace. Beckoning our Brothers and Sisters, our *Anam Ċara,* Home.

Questioning the wisdom of afflicting the (assumed) comfortable:

It has been said, in various ways, that the job of a minister is to "comfort the afflicted and afflict the comfortable."

What strikes me about the *"afflict the comfortable"* sentiment (Dunne, 1902) is that it was originally meant to be comical (and in reference to something entirely nonreligious), yet somehow has become a religious creed of sorts, and most often used in faith traditions when they wish to discount or suppress (and oppress) a person or group of people who may appear privileged and so deemed as not worthy of ministerial attention.

When I think of what motivates people to attend a church, no matter how "comfortable" they may appear to the onlooker, my guess is that they are there for comfort of some kind. *Perhaps hope for a future they cannot see, companionship they do not get anywhere else, or an hour of peace and inspiration in an otherwise stressful and busy life.*

> I wonder if there is wisdom in keeping this phrase in the humor category, and have our congregations go about the business of comforting everyone who carries their joys and sorrows through our doors.

Anne Lamott's essay about "The Book of Welcome" in her 2014 publication of *Small Victories: Spotting Improbable Moments of Grace* could well be the outline for a liturgical midrash that attempts to fill in the spaces left blank in the Hebrew Scriptures. In "The Book of Welcome," Lamott imagines a Bible book that was never written. She speaks of scriptures that would provide a set of guidances and assurances and principles that would create a sense of security and belonging for Earth's residents. She writes:

"The welcome book would have taught us that power and signs of status can't save us, that welcome — both offering and receiving — is our source of safety. Various chapters and verses of this book would remind us that we are wanted and even occasionally delighted in, despite the unfortunate truth that we are greedy-grabby, self-referential, indulgent, overly judgmental, and often hysterical." (*Welcome*, 15)

In her version, we would be accepted for our gifts *and* our apparent flaws. We are welcome because we Belong to each other. Lamott asserts that somehow that book *"went missing."* She muses that perhaps,

"When the editorial board of bishops pored over the canonical lists from Jerusalem and Alexandria, they arbitrarily nixed the book the states unequivocally that you are wanted, even rejoiced in." (*Welcome*, 16)

She says:

"We have to write that book ourselves."

And I say:

We have to write that book together!

And we do write that book together with every encounter of Welcome we share. We write The Book of Welcome every time we acknowledge the echo of divinity in our hearts and in our *Anam Ċara*. We write The Book of Welcome every time we gather together in response to our members' needs, hopes and dreams. We write The Book of Welcome every time we answer the call to invite and greet new ones into our spiritual family. We write The Book of Welcome every time we unite in the name of our congregations and evangelize in response to the calls of unity, and justice and standing on the side of love. We write The Book of Welcome together every time we open the doors to the churches we serve in and shape and shepherd The Beloved Community.

May we each recognize the Echo of Divinity in our hearts. May we recognize the Echo of Divinity in each other. May we recognize our Anam Ċara when we meet them. May we love them every day of our lives. And so it is on our journey together.

Living Life as a Prayer

A Blessing for Our Congregation

May this house of worship be blessed.

May this congregation be loving to each other.

May our doors remain open to welcome the stranger seeking spiritual solace and inspiration.

May we deepen our friendships in trust and in faith.

May we find peace and create peaceableness as we live into our shared values.

May we be joy-full and thoughtful, and

May we be a light of grace and a beacon of welcome to the world, and

May we remember that we

Belong to each other.

That we are The Beloved Community.

Amen and Blessed Be.

MÖBIUS LIVING

A Möbius strip or Möbius band is a surface with only one side and only one boundary. While this book does examine its specific *non-orientable* mathematical properties, we are going to explore its ruled surface qualities as they apply allegorically to our experience of life.

The Möbius theme at it simplest definition is talking about *inside out things*. For instance, consider what is inside an orange. If you squeeze an orange – what do you get? Orange juice. Likewise with pretty much everything. There are no surprises. If you put a carrot into a juicer, you are not going to see grape juice come out. You will get carrot juice. The same when you squeeze an orange: orange juice; lemons: lemon juice. The same is true of us – humans! When you squeeze us, metaphorically, what's inside us is revealed.

When looking specifically at a Möbius, it looks like it has two sides yet actually, it only has one side. If an ant were to crawl along the length of this strip, it would return to its starting point having traversed the entire length of the strip on both sides of the original paper without ever crossing an edge. One way to test this theory is to take your index finger and begin tracing on the inside of the ring. Your finger seems to be on the outside of the ring. It's somewhat of an optical illusion, yet you soon discover as you trace around it with your finger it really only has one side. More than an inside and an outside, what looks like its inner and outer surfaces flow into each other seamlessly, co-creating the whole. And, we humans, we are like that too.

Whatever is inside of us continually flows outward.

Whatever is outside us continually flows inward.

If what is inside us is gratitude, thoughtfulness, peace and kindness, that is what we will send out. And if those around us are grateful, kind, peaceful and thoughtful, that is what will be given to us.

What about when the things on the outside, aren't so nice? Sometimes people can say or do mean things, or sad things happen, sometimes bad things happen, sometimes we will feel pressured or squeezed, then what? Well, I believe that if we practice every day to cultivate gratitude, thoughtfulness and thanks-giving, that will fill us up so much inside us, that when the outside world isn't so friendly, when we get squeezed a little by circumstances or even feel pressed by our own chattering thoughts and emotions, we will be able to meet it with gentleness and kindness because that is what is inside us. And I am confident we have the power to accomplish this if we utilize the power of our hearts. The human heart has a broadcast capacity of 2.5 watts with every beat. What an enormous energy source! According to HeartMath founder, Doc Lew Childre in his book entitled *Freeze-frame*, the heart is "our main electrical power center. Producing 2.5 watts of power, it generates 40 to 60 times more power than the brain. The heartbeat, which produces an electrical signal, can be measured at any point on the body." (*Childre, 28*)

With every beat of our heart we can focus our attention on benevolent thoughts and actions, and we can send this signal out to those around us as well for our heartbeat acts as a communication pathway inside our bodies, and to the outer world also.

Another important distinction to consider about a Möbius is you can begin at any point because it goes on perpetually. You can start your practice where ever you are. It's easiest to begin when you are already feeling good about something. But, if your upset about something, you can circle on inward with the intention of creating peace-of-mind, calmness, and finding things to be grateful for even if they are not immediately obvious on the outside, you can build them on the inside. With practice.

I like to encourage people of all ages to practice connecting with the Möbius during a heart-based meditation. One is inspired by what I believe to be a Möbius-esque Meditation called "Breathe in Peace" by the song of Musician Sarah Dan Jones. The words are simple: "Breathe in, Breathe out" accompanied by: "When I breathe in, I breathe in peace. When I breathe out, I breathe out love." (*Jones*)

The meditations I lead with groups vary depending on size, and sometimes individuals, is this:

Place your hand in the vicinity of your heart, where you can feel the vibration of your voice and hum for a moment. Allow your gaze to soften. Slowly say the words: "Breathe in, Breathe out." Repeat them methodically several times to ground you: "Breathe in, Breathe out." Then when you have the rhythm, add these words as harmony, "When I breathe in, I breathe in peace. When I breathe out, I breathe out love." *Repeat the harmony over several times and then conclude by reciting the opening words, "Breathe in, Breathe out."*

When there are large groups, I may have one side of the room recite "Breathe in, Breathe out" while the other side chants the harmony, "When I breathe in, I breathe in peace. When I breathe out, I breathe out love."

I have come across several songs that have noticeably Möbius tenors to them such as *"Swimming to the Other Side"* by Pat Humphries and *"All Along The Watchtower"* by Bob Dylan. I have used both in sermons and retreats to demonstrate and lead participants to notice that no matter where the lyrics begin they wrap around to include all the content. The listener can hear how the story of the flows and consider if it stays true to the original intent even though it seems to be arranged differently.

For example, here are Dylan's words in Möbius arrangement:

> "All along the watchtower, princes kept the view;
>
> While all the women came and went, barefoot servants, too.
>
> Outside in the cold distance a wildcat did growl;
>
> Two riders were approaching, and the wind began to howl.
>
> 'There must be some way out of here' *said the joker to the thief,*

The Theology of Rev. Twinkle Marie Manning

There's too much confusion' I can't get no relief.

Businessmen, they drink my wine, plowmen dig my earth.

None of them along the line know what any of it is worth.'

'No reason to get excited' *the thief he kindly spoke,*

There are many here among us who feel that life is but a joke.

But you and I, we've been through that,

and this is not our fate;

So let us stop talking falsely now, the hour is getting late.'"

(Dylan)

And below are Humphries lyrics Möbius-style that lend to the theme of this book, namely the universal connection we share:

"I am alone and I am searching,

hungering for answers in my time.

I am balanced at the brink of wisdom.

I'm impatient to receive a new sign.

I move forward with my senses open.

Imperfection it be my crime.

In humility, I will listen

we're all swimming to the other side.

On this journey through thoughts

and feelings
binding intuition, my head, my heart
I am gathering the tools together.
I'm preparing to do my part.
All of those who have come before me
band together and be my guide.
Loving lessons that I will follow,
we're all swimming to the other side.
When we get there we'll discover
All the gifts we've been given to share
Have been with us since life's beginning
and we never noticed they were there.
We can balance at the brink of wisdom,
never recognizing we've arrived.
Loving spirits will live together,
we're all swimming to the other side.
We are all living beneath the great big dipper
We are all washed by the very same rain
We are swimming in this stream together
Some in power and some in pain.
We can choose to worship this ground
we walk on
Cherishing the beings that we live beside
Loving spirits will live together
We're all swimming to the other side."

(Humphries)

Those familiar with the songs will notice that the first few lines were actually the last of the original lyrics wrapping around the the beginning of the the way the song was originally laid out.

These songs I selected as well for their content and indication of a more in-depth look at how life as a Möbius can be lived. The themes in these songs play out in many of our day-to-day lives.

When life provides us with a challenge, when we see something emerging that scares us or the rug seems to have been pulled out from beneath us, we can feel like we have to begin all over again. However, I would like to suggest that that is almost never the case. That instead each step of our journey builds upon those before it, and those yet to come. That, as the Thief reminded the Joker, we are not new at this, collectively, and individually as adults, we've been doing *life* for a long time. And we know that when darkness falls and the winds begin to howl, eventually they will subside. The landscape may be rearranged by the wind and others on their journeys may have left their marks both beautiful and otherwise, leaving the environment around us looking less familiar, but the "how to" navigate is consistent. Once you've lived a certain number of years – you can begin to see your life, and life around you, has recognizable patterns.

In some ways this shouldn't surprise us. Many of us are familiar with the cycles of the moon, we recognize the seasons as they shift one to the other. There is a rhythm that is consistent with what we have come to be comfortable with, even if we don't like the cold of winter, or the heat of summer, we accept them for what they are and adapt. It is in our ability to not just adapt, but to also prepare, that enables the journey, even in the most difficult and unfamiliar passages, to unfold with more ease and peace of mind.

A Möbius strip in song, poem, or practice can begin at any place for its content has continuity. You can start at the first sentence, anywhere throughout, or even last stanza and then wrap it around and it flows, its story unfolding as clearly as if you began it from the assumed beginning. Assumed beginning because there are alot of things that come into play before Once Upon a Time. There is a history of what came before the perceived beginning of each chapter of our story, what led up to it, and also, the places it will lead us to.

If we can view the content of our life as a Möbius, or perhaps its more familiar display, as an infinity configuration, we can begin to understand that the context of our life is more than this moment, yet this moment often becomes the most important or at least the focal point, because it is where we are, and we can forget that the full context of our life includes the before and the afterward.

If we can view our life not merely moment by moment or verse by verse, and rather within the scope of the full story of our lives, we may well find that our interpretations about circumstances and events become more accurate.

I encourage you to also consider that the practices we cultivate directly influence our perceptions and impact how we respond to our experiences.

There is also alot of room for misinterpretation if we only look at a piece of a puzzle. For instance, there is a sentence found in a very well known book that states unequivocally:

"There is no God." (*Psalm* 14:1)

That book is <u>The Bible</u>. The sentence is found in the first verse of 14th Psalm. If that was the only sentence of the bible you read, you would have a perception about the book that is contrary to what the entire rest of the book says. Because the content and context of the book contain a fuller explanation than one sentence selected at random or with intention ever could. Likewise with our lives.

Most of our present moments can be summed up in one sentence or even a few words:

- They started a business.
- He lost his job.
- They got married.
- My loved one died.
- Birth of a baby
- Graduated college
- Diagnosed with an illness
- She won the lottery.
- They fell in love.
- They built a new home.

The list goes on. Yet there is more to each of these moments. They are always within the context of our lives, not isolated and so influenced by the whole.

What came before informs how you respond, and how you respond will determine the path to what comes next.

So when we are faced with something, really anything, we can be assured that we are meeting ourselves on this path of life with all the experience we have, and will have. We can draw from those experiences, positioning ourselves to weather any storm.

I recently came across a story retold by Rev. Bridget Spain of the Dublin Unitarian Church from Mitch Albom's book *"Have a Little Faith."* He received the story in his youth from his Rabbi Albert Lewis. It is called: *"John Sleeps Well in a Storm."*

The story goes basically like this:

> *A farmer was in need of help tending his farm. He lived alone, having been widowed for some time and was getting on in years. His children were all grown and have moved far away and so the farmer lived alone way out in the country. The work of keeping up the farm was beginning to take its toll on him. He loved his home, loved his farm and wanted to maintain it. But he really really needed help.*
>
> *He put out ads but because it was so far out in the country he did not get very many responses. Finally the farmer received a response from a young man. So he interviewed him and discovered the man to be very quiet. The farmer asked him,*
>
> *"Do you know how to cut hay?"*

The Theology of Rev. Twinkle Marie Manning

John said, "Yes."

"Do you know how to sow barley?"

John said, "Yes."

"Do you know how to look after cattle?"

John said, "Yes."

That's all he could get out of John. So he asked if there was anyone that John used to work for that could give him a reference so he could determine if John actually had the experience, if he was good at farming, and quite importantly: if he was trustworthy.

John said yes indeed had a reference, and a letter soon arrived to the farmer. The letter, as letters of recommendation go, was very short. It came from another farmer several townships away simply said,

"John sleeps well in a storm."

This short sentence did not make alot of sense to the farmer. But after scratching his head and wondering on it for a short while, since there were no others applying for the job and since the farmer really really needed help desperately, he decided to give John a try and hired him and gave him a small cabin on the property to live in.

Now John continued to be very quiet as he went about his work.

And he was only there a short while, about a week, when a big storm was forecasted and *the farmer was curious how it would go.*

The storm came late in the evening and the farmer was quite anxious, becoming more so as the wind got louder and louder, and the rain beating on the window, and then flashes of light, and loud booms of thunder that he was worried may startle the animals. Concerned, the farmer decided to check on things, and to get John to help him. He went outside and knocked on John's door. Not a sound from John. He knocked again but couldn't wake him.

So the farmer went around the farm checking on things himself. And he discovered that everything was very tidy. When he went to the barn, the doors were all closed. When he went to the hay shed, the hay was all carefully tied down, the grain was dry. The animals were carefully put in their stalls. Everything was secure and as it should be.

(Albom, as retold by Rev. Porter-Manning)

Suddenly the farmer knew what the reference letter meant. Because John, as was his practice, had done everything he should have done to prepare carefully, mindfully, for the forecasted storm he could rest peacefully knowing everything would be ok. Like John, if we tend to the things that are important in life, if we are right with those we love and behave in line with our faith, our lives will not be filled with restlessness or aching feelings of incomplete work. And it works both ways.

John, he prepared on the outside, so he could rest easy on the inside. We can prepare inside, so we can be equipped for whatever life has to offer outside of us. And we can be ready to greet Life with our innermost truth and gifts. If we cultivate hearts filled with love, filled with gratitude, we will have these at the ready so that in both bright and dark days we can experience these, and share these with others. If we mindfully prepare ourselves in this way, we will be better equipped to respond in loving ways, rather than to react out of fear.

As Mitch concludes,

"If we tend to the things that are important in life, if we are right with those we love, and behave in line with our faith, our lives will not be cursed with the aching throb of unfulfilled business. Our words will always be sincere, our embraces will be tight. We will never wallow in the agony of 'I could have, I should have'. We can sleep in a storm." (*Albom*, 93)

The Möbius wrapping around is an indication of the infinite loop and so it is with life.

Whatever is inside of us continually flows outward.

Whatever is outside us continually flows inward.

If life on the outside is presenting things to be grateful for, gather the gratitude for those into your Heart's storehouse. If life on the outside is presenting things that cause you to feel fear or sadness, *reach into your heart* and find the place where your love and your gratitude and your peace and peace of mind resides and bring that forward, because the world needs it. *You* need it.

Living Life as a Prayer

There is a Benediction from one of the congregations I've served, First Parish in Concord, MA, that beautifully acknowledges living life in a way that exemplifies the practice of Möbius living,

"Go out into the world in peace,

have courage,

hold on to what is good,

return to no person evil for evil,

strengthen the faint-hearted,

support the weak,

help the suffering,

honor all beings."

(Benediction)

Möbius Living teaches to be grateful for the gifts you have, practice being the You you most want to be, and Trust that you can weather any storm, especially if you prepare in advance by modeling your life in the lifestyle manner you wish to experience.

MILESTONES, THRESHOLDS & RITUALS

Listen.
"Breathe in each morning the magick of Life;
Breathe out each evening deep gratitude for living.
And Listen to the Call of the Universe
in every interaction,
in every curve in the road,
in every commitment to task,
in every covenant of relationship,
in every whispered word,
in every meditation,
in every prayer,
in every song

Listen."

Immanence and Transcendence. Both. As a deist and animist I believe in and experience both. I believe the Holy to be within us and through us and beyond us. I believe that we can intentionally connect to the Divine in both mundane and transcendent

Living Life as a Prayer

ways: Rituals that ground us in the here and now of Earth-living, and rituals that open up gateways to what is beyond where we are and beyond what we can comprehend. Practical and Mysterious. Both.

During the Wheel of the Year, and throughout our journeys in this human form, we have many milestones and thresholds. I believe we should honor these in ritual. Sometimes solitary, oftentimes in community and with our families. The birth of a child, the death of a loved one, marriages, divorces, the changes of seasons and the days we count as Holy and sacred: birthdays, anniversaries, Christmas and Solstices, Lammas and Samhain and more depending on our unique family structures, cultural heritages and traditions.

There are many books and resources on rituals and holiday celebrations. Whichever days you identify as Holy, and whichever milestones and thresholds you deem worthy of your attention, I encourage you to cultivate into your family culture and your personal spiritual practices, routines, ways and means to honor such.

The appendix lists some of *The Church of Kineo's "Holy Days."* On our website and media pages and published materials we will update rituals and worship service information to model how we honor and memorialize these days. Also, throughout this book there are a variety of rituals, mantras, prayers, meditative poems, musings and blessings that can be used as spiritual tools. Some such include:

✧ Water rituals contained in the chapters: *"Coming Home"* and *"Gentle Ripples."*

✧ *"Weaving Harmony from Within the Chaos"* is a chapter dedicated to realigning your life, it includes a *Breathing Ritual* and *Harmonizing Blessing*.

✧ In *"Amalek Within"* is the Aramaic version of *Kabbalistic Cross*. Read aloud the vibration of the mantra is centering and healing.

✧ *"In Our Own Image"* has a mantra by Rev. Della Reese Lett, reflective poems by Anne Bradstreet and Ralph Waldo Emerson, and a prayer by Rev. Naomi King. Additionally there are reflective writings and musings by a number of authors, philosophers and spiritual leaders.

✧ *"Hospitality - a Pillar of Faith"* has home and community-gathering blessings.

✧ *"On Art and Centering"* concludes with a journey-blessing.

☙ **"The Beloved Community, Anam Cara & the Divine Echo"** begins with my foundational teaching of a primordial echo combined with the Celtic teaching of Soul Friends that itself, when read or spoke aloud, can be used as contemplative journeying. This chapter also contains *A Blessing of our Mirrors in Friendship* and *A Blessing for Our Congregation*.

☙ With or without our consent, our journeys result in parts of ourselves being left behind or taken by others. Should you wish to draw any of these parts back, there is a *Reclaiming Meditation* found in the chapter of this book entitled, **"Restore Us to Memory."**

☙ **"Of Awe and Grace"** depicts a meditative scene that can be reenacted on New Year's Eve or the completion of any season of your life, solitary or with a community gathering. It can be modified for the dawn of a new day, season or cycle.

☙ **"Death Changes Everything"** contains personal reflections and readings about processing raw grief, and supporting those who are grieving. Also, a guided meditation for honoring *The Dark Season*.

❧ **"Be Like the Trees"** opens with two contemplative poems, contains a life-tragedy-processing poem entitled, *"The Afterward,"* and a guided musing on how to emulate trees in our spiritual practices and life's journey.

❧ **"Love the Land You're With"** has reflective poems and grounding rituals.

In addition to what you find in this book and other texts we publish, we will also make available recommendations on other books and resources for rituals and celebrations that you may find useful as you create your family's spiritual culture, or a solitary practice that nourishes you.

IN OUR OWN IMAGE

Let us contemplate what the Holy is to us. The scriptures tell us that we, humans, are created in God's image. In this book I am suggesting that we also consider that we create God in our own image. Our god, the one of our choosing, is the one who makes us feel most comfortable in our own skin. The one who helps us reconcile with life and with death. The one, who when our faith is challenged, and when we endure great losses or sorrows: we turn to in pain; and when we experience great wonders and joys: we turn to in gratitude.

David Foster Wallace in a 2005 Commencement Speech entitled *"This is Water"* claimed:

"There is actually no such thing as atheism. There is no such thing as not worshipping. Everybody worships. The only choice we get is what to worship. And an outstanding reason for choosing some sort of God or spiritual-type thing to worship, be it Jesus Christ or Allah, Yahweh, Jehovah, the Wiccan mother-goddess or the Four Noble Truths or some infrangible/ inviolable set of ethical principles, is that pretty much anything else you worship will eat you alive." (*Wallace*)

Pretty much anything else you worship will eat you alive. What did he mean by that?

Well, it seems that if you worship allure and imperishable beauty, you will always feel ugly; worship money and whether you could live in poverty or be a millionaire it will feel like you never have enough; worship power and you will always feel weak and live in fear; worship intelligence or mastery and no matter how smart or successful you are you will always feel like a fraud.

On one level, we already know this. Through modern psychology as well as through parables and myths passed down to us through generations, religions, and lessons. Yet the trick is keeping the truth of these knowings up-front in our daily consciousness. Being present to this knowledge every day. And using this knowledge as we make our choices. David Foster Wallace says,

"The insidious thing about these forms of worship is not that they're evil or sinful; it is that they are unconscious. They are default-settings. They're the kind of worship you just gradually slip into, day after day, getting more and more selective about what you see and how you measure value without ever being fully aware that that's what you're doing. And the world will not discourage you from operating on your default-settings, because the world of men and money and power hums along quite nicely on the fuel of fear and contempt and frustration and craving and the worship of self." (*Wallace*)

He continues to say that we have,

"The freedom to be lords of our own tiny skull-sized kingdoms, alone at the center of all creation. Yet... The most precious kind of freedom - the really important kind of freedom involves attention, and awareness, and discipline, and effort, and being able truly to care about other people and to sacrifice for them, over and over, in myriad little ways, every day. That is real freedom. The alternative is unconsciousness, the default-setting."

Some call this default setting the "rat race" it becomes "the daily grind" the ruts" we get in. Others simply recognize as the inertia of their lives. The constant gnawing sense of having had and lost some infinite thing, or worse, not having ever believed that we are part of some infinite thing.

King Solomon's wisdom is documented in the Bible book of Ecclesiastes, which is kind of a manual for understanding the daily grind. Solomon, reputedly one of the wisest, wealthiest, most successful men of his time implored listeners to understand that all of those things (wisdom, wealth, success) were mere vanities and that if one should realize all the aims, hopes and aspirations of life, they would not bring satisfaction to the heart. For that to occur is through our connection with the Divine. To think and act as if this were otherwise, following our mind alone, without consideration for our heart, can only result in an unhappy, unfulfilling life.

Perhaps with that in mind, Robin Sharma, author of the 1997 book, *The Monk Who Sold His Ferrari*, has been quoted to say,

"The mind is a wonderful servant, but a terrible master." (*Sharma*, 51)

Being a slave to your unconscious default-setting is a living death. Choosing what to think. Being cognizant and aware enough to select what you pay attention to:

that's consciousness.

Sharma puts the onus on us to choose how we train our minds by continuing on to say,

"If you have become a negative thinker, this is because you have not cared for your mind and taken the time to train it to focus on the good." *(Sharma, 51)*

It takes determination and courage to train our minds. And doing so aligns us to Source, giving us power,

"The universe favors the brave. When you resolve, once and for all, to lift your life to its highest level, the strength of your soul will guide you." *(Sharma, 139)*

This takes commitment, intentional commitment to practicing Life as the way we wish to live it. To this end Sharma advises us that,

"Lack of willpower is a mental disease. If you suffer from this weakness, make it a priority to stamp it out quickly." *(Sharma, 145)*

"When you have self-control, you will have the resolve to do the things you have always wanted to do...all these things will be within your grasp when you cultivate your sleeping reserves of willpower." *(Sharma, 148)*

The Rev. Dr. Della Reese Lett, renown for her performance career as a singer and actress, and founding minister of Understanding Principles for Better Living Church (Up Church) in Los Angeles, California, provides us with a mantra to practice so as to cultivate such self-control and willpower:

"I speak no words of limitation." (*Reese*, 147)

When we are acutely aware of our human propensity for mental distraction, indeed mental destruction, and take steps to exercise self-control, we can achieve mastery of our minds, and within our hearts. With willpower we are able to create practices that serve our greater purposes and create continuity in our connection to the Divine.

Having a steadfast practice that allows you to steer yourself back when you wander, allows you to actively choose what you focus on: That's freedom. And, that is intentional worship, even if you do not recognize it by that name.

How we consciously choose to experience the Divine can determine how our life unfolds day to day. This is not to say it will determine, in some karmic way, whether we encounter injustices, grief, or suffering. To suggest that these are completely unavoidable would be grossly misleading. For I can state with certainty that every single human being has encountered sorrow, and anger, and fear. Yet, how we respond to the things that happen to us is the key to whether or not our lives feel burdensome, or worthwhile.

The Rev. Marlin Lavanhar tells us in his 2013 sermon entitled: *"Why Life is Not Fair"* that,

"'Why?' is the wrong question to why bad things happen to good people." (*Lavanhar*)

Rev. Lavanhar, who is the senior minister at *All Souls Tulsa*, knows about life not being fair. His daughter died when she was three years old. She was before that healthy, vibrant, happy. Then out of the blue she encountered a virus that for some unknown reason attacked her heart and within days she died. So I take to heart his experiencially-affirming words about Life Not Being Fair.

Again, Marlin says:

"'Why?' is the wrong question to why bad things happen to good people."

The more important question, Marlin says is,

"Because bad things happen, what are we called to do?

We don't know why and we never will."

He preaches that,

"In the face of evil and tragedy and injustice the only response that makes any sense at all is to love. We are called to love. In the midst of it all, we are called to continue to risk loving and receiving love. We are called to be instruments of love."

Marlin urges us,

"The only god to believe in is a god of love."

1 Corinthians 13:11-13, of *The Holy Bible: New International Version (NIV)*, informs us about this love, and something of the maturity that goes along with it by saying,

"When I was a child, I talked like a child, I thought like a child, I reasoned like a child. When I became an adult I put the ways of childhood behind me. For now we see only a reflection as in a mirror; then we shall see face to face. Now I know in part; then I shall know fully, even as I am fully known. And now these three remain: faith, hope and love. But the greatest of these is love." (1 *Corinthians* 13:11-13)

The author of this book, the Apostle Paul, in speaking about how our perceptions change as we mature noted we see but a dim reflection as in a mirror; then we shall see face to face. Child self to adult self. A closer look at verse 12 is revealing as it continues:

Now (as the child self) *I know in part;*

then (as the adult self) *I shall know fully, even as I am fully known.*

After childhood ways of thinking have matured, and adulthood consciousness embraced, Paul teaches as stated above in verse 13:

"And now these three remain:

faith, hope, and love; But the greatest of these is love." (1 *Corinthians* 13:13)

and he continues on with this precious and integral thought 1 Corinthians 14:1,

"Follow the way of love and eagerly desire gifts of the Spirit." (1 *Corinthians* 13:14)

Love and gifts of the Spirit. We can distract ourselves endlessly by seeking responses to the unanswerable question: WHY? Indeed we can distract ourselves with all the Whys of Life. Yes, we can consult clergy and psychics, shaman and scriptures, and we will never with certainty find the Absolute Answer. We are far bettered served, and serve others better, when bad things happen, and they will, when good things happen, and they will, to mindfully, thoughtfully, carefully choose which God we will filter these life experiences through. And consider, how can we consciously cultivate a practice that enables us to take control over decades-long default programs?

The Reverend David Ruffin during a 2015 sermon entitled *"Transcending Together"* at All Souls Church in Tulsa, Oklahoma, when talking about the Christian account of Pentecost, when hundreds were reported having received the holy spirt, his interpretation was,

"Pentecost didn't just happen, it is happening! Pentecost is happening!! Today is a day for a direct encounter with the transcendent. And so is tomorrow. And the day after that. And here is the thing. Pentecost is not passive. It is not something we can passively await. Pentecostal moments of transcendence only come when we become co-collaborators in Pentecost. Whatever transcendent event that may have happened in that early christian community, its real power is as a present-day co-created reality. That is to say: A Pentecostal Practice." (*Ruffin*)

What is a Pentecostal Practice? It is the direct transcending of the spirit. I understand that of the many reading this book, including atheist colleagues, not all are on what we could playfully call the Pentecostal "Spectrum." Many, but not all of my colleagues believe in connection to Spirit. And, even those of us who are and do, may unfortunately hesitate in owning any phrase with connotations so steeply rooted in Christianity. Yet, the faith tradition outside of *The Church of Kineo* where I most regularly have preached, Unitarian Universalism, has roots in this idea of transcendence, even if the majority their modern-day ministers do not align with such teachings. Transcendentalism for example.

The followers of Transcendentalism felt a deep calling to live lives of personal integrity and to bring about social change. Transcendentalism evolved as an organic consequence of the emphasis on free conscience and the value of intellectual reason. Yet, Transcendental philosophy was not grounded in mere physical experience, rather deriving from the inner spiritual or mental essence of the human. Indeed, Transcendentalism made personal spiritual experience and individual conscience its guides. Transcendentalists wanted a religion that allowed for a personal connection to the Divine. And, my guess is that all of us can relate to moments of feeling deep connection. Connection to Nature. Connection to other Humans. Connection to Divinity.

When we experience those connections, that is the beginning of transcendence. Often times it is *Transient* transcendence, or a passing sense of confirmation; evidence we are part of something more than what is seen. Yet, for one reason or another, it does not become our lived reality. We inevitably sink back into our patterns of being weighted down by the world, systemically or personally feeling entrenched in fears and uncomfortably, or numbly facing our daily lives. But we can choose something different. We can choose to practice transcendence. Practice. And by practicing transcendence, inasmuch as it is a solitary implementation that creates a unique feeling for each of us individually, it is also a way of being together in this world. Transcendence is a way of being in this world together. Because, whether one of us is practicing it, or all of us are, the connection is palpable.

The Theology of Rev. Twinkle Marie Manning

As Della Reese affirms,

"I am one with all the power there is. I will learn how to contact His power within me! I will learn how to cooperate with this power! I will learn how to use this power wisely. I will keep this power flowing." (*Reese*, 115)

If we each take steps day by day to hone the skills of transcendence, we strengthen not only ourselves, but our community. We strengthen our relationships with one another. Of seeing our imperfections, and greeting each other in love anyway. We say YES to the Call to be instruments of Love. And in doing so, will begin to see the world, and each other, through more authentic and compassionate lenses. And in doing this, we not only answer the call to Love, we fall in love with Life and with each other all over again.

In the 2012 novel, *A Man Called Ove*, by Fredrik Backman we are provided with a beautiful depiction of the kind of deeply-acquainted and intimately-familiar love that unfolds over long periods of time:

"Loving someone is like moving into a house. At first you fall in love with all the new things, amazed every morning that all this belongs to you, as if fearing that someone would suddenly come rushing through the door to explain that a terrible mistake had been made, you weren't actually supposed to live in a wonderful place like this. Then over time, the walls become weathered, the wood splinters here and there, and you start to love that house not so much because of all its perfection, but rather for the imperfections. You get to know all the nooks and crannies. How to avoid getting the key caught in the lock when it's cold outside.

Which of the floorboards flex slightly when one steps on them or exactly how to open the wardrobe doors without them creaking. These are the little secrets that make it your home." (*Backman*, 305)

Love. When we choose to experience it and act from it, Love has a wonder all its own. We can take heart in this when we experience the less polished sides of each other. We can choose to love each other anyway. And when our perceptions of life and living become jaded when bad things happen, we can choose love and choose faith in the Divine here as well. Because when we pause for even a moment in Nature we cannot deny that there is something *more than*, out there; and we can choose to have that knowledge have positive significance to us.

Renown Channel of the Seth Material, Jane Roberts talked about why it is important to not simply rely on default-settings but to be aware of what we think. The website for The Seth Learning Center cites her as saying:

"Whatever you habitually think sinks into the subconscious. The subconscious is the seat of the emotions and is a creative mind. Once the subconscious accepts an idea, it begins to execute it. Whatever you feel is true, your subconscious will accept and bring forth into experience." (*Roberts*)

How this relates to others Roberts says,

"You are so part of the world that your slightest action contributes to its reality. Your breath changes the atmosphere. Your encounters with others alter the fabrics of their lives, and the lives of those who come in contact with them." (*Roberts*)

She also wanted a defining factor, to that end she speaks,

"I kept looking for a logic that would explain life. It never occurred to me that instead Love is the vital synthesis." (*Roberts*)

Again. Love. And connection. Components and keys to creating The Beloved Community.

In the words of our literary and liberal religious foremother Poetess Anne Bradstreet as penned in *Contemplations* from 1679, we see ever more clearly the innate connection to the Divine through the assignment of that which is revealed by observing Nature's glory and, when we listen for it, our Soul's reaction to our undeniable connection to the Universe:

"Then higher on the glistening (glistering) sun I gaz'd,

Whose beams was shaded by the leavie tree;

The more I look'd, the more I grew amaz'd,

And softly said, What glory's like to thee?

Soul of this world, this universe's eye,

No wonder, some made thee a deity."
(*Bradstreet*)

Ralph Waldo Emerson took this sentiment to heart affirming:

"Let me go where ever I will,

I hear a sky-born music still.

It is not only in the rose,

Living Life as a Prayer

It is not only in the bird,

But in the darkest, meanest things

There always, always, something sings."
                        (*Emerson*)

Yes, we could choose to chalk their words up to fancy talk, whimsical dreams and ignore them. Indeed, we can continue on with our default-settings. Or we can choose to embrace the Divine and see where such a decision leads us. We can choose to release ourselves from the distraction of trying to solve the insolvable, and begin to live. Because, whether we like it or not, we create our personal gods in our image with every choice we make, and too with every choice we try to avoid making.

The good news is that we can choose to worship gods of benevolence, of compassion, of kindness. We can choose to worship gods of forgiveness, of transcendence, of peace. These are the gods of Love. We can choose to whom we belong. And when we choose them, we answer the call to love. And when we answer the call to love, even in the face of our imperfections, in the face of uncertainties and fears. We begin to emulate the god we created in our own image.

May the Gods we choose to create in our image give us the courage to risk loving and receiving love. While me may not ever know the "whys" of existence, and where it may take some of us great effort to mindfully realign our default-settings, as we begin cultivating transcendent practices, let us take heed of the Rev. Naomi King's prayer as posted on her website:

"Sit down beside us, Beloved, in the garden, and let us rest against your knees, that we may recount why we are thankful and how. At the end of our days, may we be thankful for all the chances to choose love and to choose hope and to choose justice and to choose generosity and to choose wonderment and to choose joy. Sit down beside us, Beloved, in this graciousness of being, and let us lean against your knees, and breathe in the yes that is and breathe out with all the love we have to give." (*King, N.*)

Let us remember this. May we ever feel our connection to each other and to all we call Sacred. Let us co-create this reality together and walk in peace wherever we are.

Living Life as a Prayer

AMALEK WITHIN

Everyday we know:

Someone's heart is breaking;

Someone's soul is soaring;

Someone's mind is racing.

We each carry with us our joys, our sorrows, our dreams, and our fears. Real or imagined. Coerced by others or self-imposed, they join us here in these pews. It is up to us to create a space so sacred and so secure so as to be able to contain it all. Holding the joys and triumphs of some in the same space and time as the sorrows and anxieties of others can be complex, especially when a heart overflowing with exaltation meets the eyes of one in despair. Yet, I believe we are up for this challenge.

Acknowledging the existence of, and allowing exploration into, uncomfortable areas to help with identifying the potential influences we are impacted by are of primary importance. These external and internal forces are with us as we go about our daily lives. Sometimes they are among our greatest assets. Other times, our worst enemy. There are words we don't hear spoken of too very much in our faith. Sin, Evil, Enemy are some such words. Perhaps an evolutionary sidestep in our strivings to create language that supports welcoming monikers. Perhaps, a shying away from, as we attempt to create an atmosphere of Universal Love, of Oneness. Good motives, yes, but it is useful to see the framework inclusive of all its parts.

Let's shed some light on the darker side of things and embark on a spiritual exploration together. Perhaps there are truths to be revealed in the mysterious tales of our cultures. Perhaps they can stand alone as metaphor enough to impact how we go about our lives.

There is a story in the Hebrew Scriptures about the tribe of Amalek. The Amalekites were said to be semi-nomadic (wanderers) and lived in the land called Moab of ancient Israel. They were cause of significant worry to the tribes of Israel at the time because the Amalekites were notorious for their sneak attacks and targeting of the most vulnerable in the Jewish communities. (*Deuteronomy* 25:17,18)

Amalekites always attacked the rear of their encampments where typically the sick, the elderly, and the children were. And, they were ferocious. Because of this, as the ancient story goes, the tribes of Israel were commanded to wipe out Amalek wherever they encountered them. (*1 Samuel* 15:18)

As time went on, it became clearer that this story was perhaps more allegory than history. Rabbi Daniel Bogard in a July 2017 social media post says, quoting a sermon he had recently delivered:

"Sages realized that Amalek wasn't an ethnic group----they were *an inclination*." (*Bogard*)

And he says that,

"In every generation, we are told, Amalek rises again, and in every generation, we are obligated to stand with the vulnerable against those who would oppress them." (*Bogard*)

At a time when we have leaders who are seeking to strip people of human rights, of dignity, of choice. At a time when countless are being denied access to health-care, to nutritious food, to living in safe homes, even some being denied access to serve our country in military service. At a time when our Earth is being desecrated, her natural resources are being pillaged, and skies are being polluted to devastating degrees because of absolute greed. I think it is safe to say Amalek has risen. And it is our obligation to protect the vulnerable from such an enemy.

Rabbi Bogard prophesied,

"In every generation Amalek returns; now is the time for our generation to stand with the vulnerable, to stand up for a more inclusive and humane world, and to push back against the evil of this Amalek." (*Bogard*)

Amalek is the prodigal enemy of freedom. The enemy of peace. And, Amalek is not just an exterior force. Amalek attacks from the inside as well. Yes, there is Amalek within each of us. The Amalek Within. It is of benefit to acknowledge this and explore its significance. Swiss psychiatrist and psychoanalyst, Carl Jung, speaks of this when he says,

"Everyone carries a shadow, and the less it is embodied in the individual's conscious life, the blacker and denser it is..... if it is repressed and isolated from consciousness, it never gets corrected." (*Jung*, 131)

Don Juan, the spiritual teacher of the Carlos Castaneda books, referred to such a dark force in a more triggering way in which he calls the internal predator. He says,

"We have a companion for life...We have a predator that came from the depths of the cosmos and took over the rule of our lives. Human beings are its prisoners. The predator is our lord and master." (*Castaneda*, 218)

Castaneda says these aliens act as mental predators, prompting destructive emotions of fear, anxiety, anger, despair, jealousy and competitiveness which create the kind of energetic qualities that feed them and give them strength and influence over us.

In the Bible, this lord and master; this ruler of the world, is called Satan the Devil, an angel turned demon bent on luring humankind away from the God of Love and causing harm to each other. An Adversary said to use temptation is its primary tool.

Another Adversary appearing in the form of a demon offering great temptation was Mara to the Buddha. Time and again, the parable of Mara stands for the tempestuous longings and fears that assail us, as well as the views and opinions that confine us to a certain kind of paralysis of body, mind and spirit. Affecting not only the psychological realm but the physical as well.

The Druids, Celtic and Norse traditions all point to

various *elemental creatures* - seen and unseen - who tempt and entice both The Goods and The Ills of our humane nature.

The Ojibwa and other indigenous peoples identify this dark force as the Wétigo or Windigo (Wendigo). Alternately, depending on the tribe, it is seen as a *virus or entity* that infects people like a parasite or spirit possession, consuming the life force of the host.

Philosopher Ralph Waldo Emerson and Mystic Eckhart Tolle are among those who refer to such distractive and destructive forces as Ego that reveal themselves in compulsive thought processes. Tolle tells us,

"The mind is incessantly looking not only for food for thought; it is looking for food for its identity, its sense of self. This is how the Ego comes into existence and continuously re-creates itself." (*Tolle*, 27)

These are but a glimpse at they types of conclusions drawn by those who have examined the reasons behind thoughts and behaviors that are in opposition to anything we call Holy, and to anything resembling that which would be considered humane, compassionate, benevolent. Indeed, around the world credence is given in virtually every culture to the idea that we are being influenced outwardly and inwardly. The key is to be aware of this. And, creatures of habit - as we humans are, it is important to create mindfulness systems that produce habits that support the ways in which we most want to think, and feel, and behave. With out such structures in place, such internal and external methods practiced and honed, we can easily fall prey to Amalek, to the Adversary. Jesus of the Bible cautioned us with the principle that *"no one can serve two masters."* (*Matthew* 6:24)

In the book of Matthew, where he is quoted as stating this, he was talking about the love of money being an injurious thing. We can carry this sentiment over to any of the ills of our human nature. We can vanquish the ill, or at least minimize its negative impact by First identifying the dark side of human nature, not just the dark side, but our dark sides, individually and collectively. Name it. Clarify it.

Greed, for instance: Hunger is not greed and greed is not hunger. Hunger is satisfied when it is nourished. Greed is only satisfied while it is consuming. Whether feeding hunger or fueling greed, we actively impact ourselves and each other. And we do so in myriad ways. Physically – with choices that help or hinder life on our planet. Energetically – by thoughts and actions that create harmony or disharmony.

The reaction to Amalek is typically one directional: blaming someone else, or blaming ourselves. The cost is high either way, so it is crucial to understand the didactic evidence of the deep roots of Amalek, and once aware, to take the time to mindfully consider what to do with such knowledge. How to potentially dissolve or at least disrupt Amalek's cycles of influence.

Like the story of Jesus, who was approached by the Adversary while fasting in the wilderness, Buddha too was most often approached by Mara while alone, meditating or fasting. These accounts remind us to be aware that during the times when we are focused on positive things does not prevent negative influences from challenging us. Indeed, as we strive towards positive changes in our lives, we can count on encountering challenges. There are also accounts of Mara approaching the Buddha while he was instructing his students and when he was addressing large gatherings, and even when doing the seemingly mundane tasks of any given day. Reminding us that such Adversaries can seek to distract us at any given moment of the day or night, with thoughts that sound like our own voices, or the voices of those we can be most influenced by. And even with dreams that mislead.

The Wétigo and the Predator, too, instilling feelings of fear or numbness that distract us from the good that is with us. Such feelings taking away our sense of purpose as swiftly as they consume our energy. In many ways, like the tribes of Israel, we live in exile. We go about our lives feeling disconnected to each other, disconnected to source, disconnected to a sense of purpose.

We, each of us, have our own version of Amalek that we carry with us. A burden that precipitates, and simultaneously emphasizes, the effect of Amalek. Oh, Amalek is easy to identify on the outside! Amalek in the form of a president or king who is selfish and greedy and seeks to cause harm to whole nations of people, yes, that is easy to identify. But Amalek on the inside? Who often masquerades as our own voice? Convincingly persuading us away from our Heart's desire? And Soul's purpose? That, yes, that, can be more difficult to recognize.

To unmask The Amalek Within takes practice. To vanquish Amalek, if possible, *takes faith*. For many of us that faith, that confidence begins with the first source from which we draw faith and wisdom from. Namely, direct experience of that transcending mystery and wonder, affirmed in all cultures, which moves us to a renewal of the spirit and an openness to the forces which create and uphold life. Emerson spoke to us about just such a force when he described the function of the Over-Soul, reflecting on the divine nature of the human soul, as connected to the collective consciousness of the Universe. One of the key attributes to the Over-Soul is the connection of the Human Soul to the Soul of God. And to this we have access to at all times, for we are part of it, even as it is part of us. (*Emerson*)

Whether we accept the idea that there are nefarious unseen forces influencing us internally and externally; or we view the symbol of Amalek as the personification of our greatest fears; or even simply a result of human brain chemistry and hormones causing errant (or sometimes perpetual) negative thoughts and feelings; storms of our own minds' makings. We can take heart that we are not alone in these experiences of the darker sides of our nature. For this is a burden we each carry. We can know, too, that we have places to turn to help build resilience, especially when we are feeling vulnerable.

One thing that we can each do, is to begin a practice of resetting our thoughts and feelings when we recognize them as adversarial, non-beneficial. I am talking specifically about the inner-critic. You know - - - the thoughts that tell us that we are not good enough. The berating thoughts; the thoughts that distract us from what brings us the most joy. And the thoughts that assign us as judge and critic of others. These are the Amalek within, sneaking up on us, attacking us from the inside when we are most vulnerable or when we are not prepared and easily distractable. Often they are quiet, tiptoeing in unnoticed at first. When you find yourself detouring along the paths of such thoughts, know that you can instantly dissolve their impact by observing them, and change your direction by steering toward positive thoughts.

Likewise with *feelings,* that are often even more powerful than thoughts. Once we notice ourselves sinking into feelings of despair, we are in a position to redirect them. That is not say we want to invalidate our emotions. It is ok, even healthy, to allow ourselves to feel our sadness. But to be consumed by sadness, to allow anxiety and fear to cripple us is unnecessary. One effective way to move our thoughts and feelings into the directions we want is to Move Our Bodies and our Voices.: go for a run; walk your dog; do yoga or stretches; sing; dance, even if you are alone in your kitchen - Dance. Move Your Body and your thoughts and feelings will follow.

But there is something even more important than learning such self-discipline. In fact, it can give you the courage and strength to create healthy new patterns. Rev. Ian White Mayer's first and foremost solution to every challenge is:

"To Invite God In." (*Maher*)

He says that,

"Once I've called myself to rest in the spiritual place, then the other solutions appear."

This is a form of surrender that we can find quite uncomfortable, at first. Especially when we, as a non-creedal faith tradition without doctrines, have an ambiguous interpretation of God. But, my guess is, that we each have something that we feel is Holy. And I urge you to turn to that first. When feeling vulnerable; when feeling scared, when feeling like you are just not quite feeling like yourself, turn to that which you identify as Holy, identify as Sacred.

And, if I may suggest:
Surrender to that.
And, by "surrender," I mean - *Pray*.

And here is the thing: Prayer can be as diverse as our interpretations of that which we call Holy.

Prayer can be found in stillness: Intentionally being still. Being silent. Sitting in your home, or at the river, or ocean, or lake. In the midst of a forest. In Sunshine or Starshine or Rain.

Prayer can be your voice: chanting as you are drawing down the moon, or singing a lullaby to your child, or to yourself.

Prayer can be visualization: envisioning that which you wish to be made manifest; seeing and focusing in your mind your fondest dreams and most heartfelt desires.

Prayer can be the act of writing: a poem or words written in stream of consciousness.

Prayer can be expressions of Deep Gratitude:

> "*Abundant Earth Mother, thank you for the nourishment you provide us each day.*" (*Manning*)

> "Thank you Father for Your unspeakable gifts. Thank you that I am enriched in every phase of my life." (*Reese, 153*)

Prayer can be pleas for help, and for guidance:

"Dear God, I don't know how I am going to face what is next, please help me see the path that is mine to take, and instill in me the courage to take it."

Prayer can be a blessing or mantra:

"Ah-teh, Mal-Kooth, Vay-Gay-Boo-Rah, Vay-Ga-Doo-Lah, Le-Olam, Ah-men"

Translated as:

"Though Art within me, The Kingdom, And the Power, And the Glory, Forever Amen." (*Druidic*, 5)

Prayer can be a single word, simply felt or thought and released to the Divine in a silent whisper:

"Love."

May we surrender to prayer and make it our daily practice to use its powerful energy, because:

Every day we know:

Someone's heart is breaking;

Someone's soul is soaring;

Someone's mind is racing;

Let us together remember to create the space to hold all this and create a world of hope and blessing through prayer. May it be so. Amen.

Love Enough

"To love without knowing how to love wounds the person we love." I repeat, "To love without knowing how to love wounds the person we love."

These words attributed to Zen Buddhist Teacher Thich Nhat Hanh resonate fully in his book *True Love: A Practice for Awakening the Heart* published in 2006 by Shambhala, may well explain the mystery of how we can profess love for one another yet continue to experience pain. In this book Hanh speaks of Avalokiteshvara, a bodhisattva who has the ability to listen and to understand others. Hanh claims that the root of human suffering lies in not being truly loved, more specifically meaning: not being listened to and understood. He encourages us that we each have the power to connect with each other at this level of true loving that embodies deep listening and understanding, but that it takes commitment and practice, elsewise the suffering will perpetuate. (Hanh, 37)

While love may be thought to be one of the most quintessential capacities of the human condition, indeed, much of our faith leads us to believe it is the core of, and goal of, our existence, it is also very much a learned dynamic interaction that improves resonance with deliberate practice and focused attention. True Love is active, it is a communion, a covenant.

The song, *Nature Boy*, released in 1948 by Nat King Cole persuades us to a better understanding of the most important gift that Love is:

"There was a boy;

A very strange enchanted boy.

They say he wandered very far, very far,

Over land and sea.

A little shy and sad of eye,

But very wise was he.

And then one day,

A magic day he passed my way.

And while we spoke of many things,

Fools and kings,

This he said to me:

'The greatest thing you'll ever learn,

Is just to love and be loved in return.'

The greatest thing you'll ever learn,

Is just to love and be loved in return." (*Cole*)

Sufi poet and philosopher Khalil Gibran spoke of the necessities and boundaries of love in his poem, *"Love One Another"*:

"Let there be spaces in your togetherness,

And let the winds of the heavens dance between you.

Love one another, but make not a bond of love:

Let it rather be a moving sea between the shores of your souls.

Fill each other's cup but drink not from one cup.

Give one another of your bread but eat not from the same loaf

Sing and dance together and be joyous, but let each one of you be alone,

Even as the strings of a lute are alone though they quiver with the same music.

Give your hearts, but not into each other's keeping.

For only the hand of Life can contain your hearts.

And stand together yet not too near together:

For the pillars of the temple stand apart,

And the oak tree and the cypress grow not in each other's shadow." (*Gibran*)

Humanist Philosopher Erich Fromm, in his 1956 book, *The Art of Loving,* tells us:

"To love is to lose control. Paradoxically, the ability to be alone is the condition for the ability to love. Lovers need to know how to lose themselves and then how to find themselves again." (*Fromm,* 112)

He affirms,

"Love is primarily giving, not receiving. Love is a decision, it is a judgment, it is a promise. If love were only a feeling, there would be no basis for the promise to love. A feeling comes and it may go. Love requires discipline, concentration, patience, faith, and the overcoming of narcissism. It isn't a feeling, it is a practice." (*Fromm*, 56)

Yes, he says that love is an activity, not a passive affect; it is a "standing in," not a "falling for." (*Fromm*, 22)

Love is not a resting place, but moving, growing, working together; when there is harmony or conflict, joy or sadness. Fromm, in his experienced perspectives as a psychologist, psychoanalyst and sociologist, concludes,

"Mature love is union under the condition of preserving one's integrity, one's individuality; a power which breaks through the walls which separate, which unites with each other others; love overcomes the sense of isolation and separateness. Infantile love follows the principle:

'I love because I am loved.'

Mature love follows the principle:

'I am loved because I love.'

Immature love says:

'I love you because I need you.'

Mature love says:

'I need you because I love you.'" (*Fromm*, 20)

What a perfect sentiment for portraying Love in a mindful Möbius setting. A Möbius Love does not deny its need for another, neither does it place false attachments on such Love. Möbius Living calls us to acknowledge Love's place in our lives. Love exists as nourishment. It exists as an active energetic force that confirms our connection to those we Love. And, once that connection is recognized, it is easy to release pretenses of self-sufficiency that keep us separated from Love, from Unity.

Antonio Carlos Jobim carved out a melodic tune in 1967 that brought full meaning to the definition and actualities of Love in his song, *"Wave"* when he pointed to the fact that the awareness of Truth that our hearts unequivocally know, and that is that:

> "The fundamental loneliness goes
> Whenever two can dream a dream together." (*Jobim*)

The guise of separation, perpetuated by our individual strivings towards an ego-based self-sufficiency, often dubbed as empowerment methods of law-of-attraction, can have the negating effect of having us believe that we are, indeed, self-sufficient, and that attaining self-sufficiency is a primary goal of our Soul's enlightenment. I believe this to be false and that the perpetuation of such teachings to be harmful to the individual and to the human experience as a whole. As Jobim, and so many others have pointed out, when two (or more) dream a dream together, authentic success is achieved. This is because our fundamental nature is that of being connected to one another. Whether in romantic relationships or within the realm of the fuller Beloved Community, we are meant to nurture our connections, not separate from them.

For as long as we have had words to speak, we have used them to capture subjective definitions of love.

According to Roman Krznari's 2013 article in *Yes! Magazine,* as well as and other easily found sources, the Ancient Greeks had six definitive kinds of love –

and within some of them, even more specific kinds. Eros, Philia, Ludus, Agape, Philautia, and Pragma. (*Krznari*)

Eros, named after the Greek god of fertility, represented sexual passion and intense desire. E*ros* was often viewed as a dangerous manifestation of love as it was perceived as a fiery and irrational, you were at risk of losing control of your senses. which frightened the Greeks.

Philia/*Phileo*¯, described deep friendship, a companionable love, camaraderie and loyalty and trust.

Ludus, was for the gift of play, the idea of playful love, such as the affection between children and new friends.

Agape Love. Perhaps most radical, *agape* or selfless love. A love that one extended to all people, regardless of family or friend relation, most often designated to strangers. *Agape* was later translated into Latin as *caritas*, which is the origin of our word "charity." Said to be highest form of Christian love – or in our case Faith-originated love.

Philautia, was love of the self and of this variety of love Greeks realized there were two types: An unhealthy version associated with narcissism, where one became self-obsessed and focused perhaps on personal fame and fortune and most certainly self-interest. And, a healthier love that enhanced one's capacity to love. An interpretation to be that if you like yourself and feel secure in yourself, you will have the ability to give love to others.

Pragma meant longstanding love. This, the mature love – the deep understanding that developed between long-married couples, long-time partners. *Pragma* was about making an effort to give love rather than just receive it making compromises to help the relationship work over time, and showing patience and tolerance. Erich Fromm observed that we expend too much energy on "falling in love" and need to learn more how to "stand in love." *Pragma* is the awareness and practice of standing in love.

In Hebrew we find four words for love, but they are not always translated as love.

Ahav (love),

Racham (tender mercies – a romantic love)

Dodi (beloved as spousal love), and

Ra'ah (brotherly love, or friendship).

During the Babylonian exile, Aramaic became the language spoken by the Jews, and Aramaic square script replaced the Paleo-Hebrew alphabet. After the Achaemenid Empire captured Babylon, Aramaic became the language of culture and learning. In the Aramaic Bible is the word *Chav*. *Chav* is similar to the Hebrew word *Ahav* to mean *love*, but, their definitions are different.

The key difference between the words, is that *Chav* is a love that is not necessarily returned. *Chav* is speaking of a love that flows from just one person and is not completed. As pointed out in the book, "Hebrew Word Study: Revealing The Heart Of God" by Chaim Bentorah:

"For love to be completed, it must be returned. Love can be lonely and painful if it is not returned." (*Bentorah*)

The Hebrew *Racham* is a completed love. This is true love.

With these in mind, we could perhaps summarize a *Biblical Cliff's Notes to the Corinthians* with:

Cliff's Notes to the Corinthians

Love is patient.

Love is kind.

Love is intensely passionate, yet

Love is not easily angered.

Love is deeply affectionate.

Love is loyal.

Love always protects.

Love always trusts.

Love one another;

Love one another.

Looking beyond Judeo-Christian roots, we find verbal applications of love in languages around the world. We are told that Sanskrit has ninety-six words for love. 96! I am *not going to list every one of them :)*

Instead, I will point to Thich Nhat Hanh in his wisdom-filled way as delineates a concise enumeration of the essence of these — by relating to us Buddhism's Four Aspects of true love, translated as: loving-kindness or benevolence, compassion, joy, and equanimity or freedom.

He tells us that true, authentic, unconditional love becomes possible when we practice cultivating these four aspects. He explains that the first aspect is metta or *maitri*. Translated as loving-kindness or benevolence, metta is a gentle love signifying the good-natured, kind-hearted feeling we have for a close friend. This idea of loving-kindness and benevolence is more than the desire to make someone happy; it is the *ability* to do so. The ability to bring joy and happiness to the person you love.

The second element of true love is called *karuna, translated as* compassion. Again more than the desire to ease the pain of another person, but more fully: the *ability* to do so. While the word karuna is generally translated as "compassion," which literally means to "suffer with," it is good to note that we don't need to suffer ourselves in order to alleviate the suffering of another person. Doctors and nurses, for instance, do not have to suffer illness in order to relieve their patients' pain. Ministers and Spiritual Leaders do not have to take on the emotional pain of their parishioners. The ability to heal comes with knowledge and understanding, which are always at the root of the practice. Thich Nhat Hanh tells us *deep looking* is needed,

"You must practice *deep looking* directed toward the person you love. Because if you do not understand this person, you cannot love properly." (*Hanh*, 2)

Mudita is the third element of true love and means "joy." Joy must exist or it is not true love. If you are in a relationship while suffering all the time and crying in sadness often, or if you make the person you claim to love suffer or cry in sadness often, it is not true love. That is not to say there are no tears or sadness or even discomforts in love. Yet amid all emotions, True Love seeks to generate joy and nurture it. More than that, true love has the power to heal and transform sadness into joy.

The fourth aspect of true love is *upeksha*, meaning equanimity or freedom. This is the love of commitment and of covenant. It is a love of devotion in the truest sense. In true love, you attain freedom. When you love with devotion, you bring freedom to the person you love. If the opposite is true, it is not true love.

Thich Nhat Hanh urges us to understand that:

"You must love in such a way that the person you love feels free, not only outside but also – inside. A good question – a wise question – for testing out whether your love is something real is: 'Dear one, do you have enough space in your heart and all around you?'" (Hanh, 4)

Dear one do you have enough space in your heart and all around it? Yes, true love listens deeply to that answer. The Key to whether or not it is true love is found in the Response of the Questioner, once the question is answered. If the one you love says I have not enough space I need more freedom, true love responds with more freedom. If the one you love says I have too much space I need more closeness, true love responds with more closeness. Anytime the response is different it is not true love; it is ego taking the lead trying to direct a space it has no place or ability to do anything other than cause damage in.

As cited above, Thich Nhat Hanh tells us, *"To love without knowing how to love wounds the person we love."* Loving-kindness, Compassion, Joy, Freedom these are the traits of love. It is not merely our desire to give and receive these elements, it is our ability to do so that constitutes real love.

The Four Measurables of Buddhism in relation to love could well be:

Love creates freedom and clarity.

Love creates safety and comfort.

Love creates peace and unity.

Love creates happiness and its manifestations.

A key to Love is Deep Listening and Learning to Speak with Love Again. Practicing loving speech is essential. To act in loving ways is essential. To achieve loving in words and deeds, we need to look deeply into the nature of our suffering and our joy. We must learn also to recognize the suffering and joy in those we love. Understanding someone's suffering is one of the bests gift we can give another person. If we do not understand, we cannot love.

What of the practice of loving?

A key is to understand

the importance of *knowing* how the person you love

wants to be loved,

and having the person you love

know how you want to be loved,

and somehow,

together,

learning how to love each other

so that you both *feel loved.*

This takes commitment.

It takes understanding.

It takes practice.

And when this is achieved:

Trust is fortified.

But how?

How can we learn to love our partners in a way that they will feel our love? How can we teach our partners to love us so that we feel loved?

Gary Chapman, in his 1995 book, *"The Five Love Languages: How to Express Heartfelt Commitment to Your Mate,"* describes five ways we express and experience love. He says it is crucial to understand both our own preferred love languages, and the preferred love languages of those we love. We can heal past hurts and create healthy, happy futures with our loved ones in direct proportion to how we responsibly and mindfully choose to incorporate loving practices into our lives. He tells us,

"We are creatures of choice...Love doesn't erase the past, but it makes the future different. When we choose active expressions of love in the primary love language of (the one we love) we create an emotional climate where we can deal with our past conflicts and failures. (*Chapman,* 131)

According to the Chapman's theory, each person has primary and secondary love languages. These are our preferred ways of experiencing love. Of receiving love.

The five love languages are:

– Words of Affirmation: Expressing affection through spoken words speaking of praise, appreciation, fondness, passion, endearments and sentiments.

– Acts of Service: Actions, rather than words, are used to show and receive love.

– Receiving Gifts: Gifting is symbolic of love and affection.

– Quality Time: Expressing affection with undivided, undistracted attention.

– Physical Touch: With this love language, the affection is felt through physical touch. It can be sex or holding hands. (*Chapman, 119*)

Each of us assign priority ranking to these love languages. We are happiest and feel most loved when we experience love regularly by way of our primary love language preference. Our joy seeps away when we do not receive love in the way we need it most. Most of us are familiar with the studies that point to babies who do not receive love die. Some of us too, know of the "silent nurseries" where babies born into war-torn and poverty-stricken locales living in orphanages without sufficient staff to care for them learn in infancy – there is no sense in crying because no one responds. So, they stop crying. All of them. What an eery sound of silence that must be.

In similar ways, as adults, when our needs for love go unanswered, *we shut down*. If, for instance, our primary love language is *Physical Touch* and we go days, or weeks or more without a hug, or holding hands, or a caress, our heart wilt.

If, our primary love language is *Words of Affirmation*, and we rarely if ever receive affectionate words, and are not told, *"You are important to me," "I adore you,"* and *"I love you,"* our heart carries aching wounds.

If *Quality Time* is our primary love language, and the person we love is too busy with work and other distractions to honor our need for dedicated time together, our hearts become sorrow-filled.

When our needs are not met we experience feelings of rejection, of sadness, of loneliness. We feel unloved. And, even unlovable. And, the reality is that many times this is not an accurate reflection of those we love not loving us.

Rather, it is that we collectively do not understand the need to understand each other. And the importance of acting according to what we discover about each other.

True Love Listens Deeply!
True Love Responds Lovingly!

When we discover what the love language is of someone we love, *True Love responds with that love language*. But, we may wonder, what if the primary love language of the person we love is difficult for us to express? This is where we return to the Four Aspects of Love in Thich Nhat Hanh's teachings and look inside our own hearts to discover if we have effectively cultivated the ability to embody True Love, and where we may need more practice. The desire, inclination, and ability to love the person we love *in the way in which they most want to Be Loved* is the test of True Love.

"Dear one, do you have enough space in your heart and all around you?" (*Hanh*, 4)

Are we prepared to ask this question to who we love, for it begs an answer for which we must be ready to respond to. Romantic love, yes, but also let's extend this to all those we feel called to love. Our children. Our parents. Our siblings. Our friends. Our neighbors. And those in our wider communities. In the apostle Paul's first letter to the Corinthians, he concludes:

"And now these three remain: faith, hope and love. But the greatest of these is love." (1 Corinthians 13:13)

He is referring to Agape Love. Charity and our ability to care for strangers. As we move towards building The Beloved Community we are covenanted to be ambassadors of such Love.

When we feel called to extend love to others, a person or a group in need of our love, it would behoove us to pause first, rather than be led by assumptions, and instead ask,

"Dear one, do you have enough space in your heart and all around you?" (*Hanh*, 4)

or perhaps said another way,

"Dear one, how can I best demonstrate my love for you in a way that you will feel most loved?"

As we emulate the kinds of Love and Loving it will take to be builders of The Beloved Community with the practices and principles of *Living Life as a Prayer*, may we always and all ways listen deeply and respond fully.

May we remember the five love languages:

- Words of Affirmation
- Acts of Service
- Receiving Gifts
- Quality Time
- Physical Touch

Let us learn how to *love enough*. Let us create the space for deep listening with those we love. Let us have the courage to ask for the love we need in order to thrive. Let us *love each other enough* to respond to such requests.

For, the greatest thing we will ever learn,
is just to love and be loved in return.

UNDOUBTED LOVE: A MATTER OF TRUST

Learning how to love and be loved in return, also means learning how to *trust* and be trusted in return. While I affirm there exists a place in our hearts where intimacy has no limit and love has no barrier, I believe that place is sacred and is meant to be accessed by-invitation-only. That invitation can be as broad or as narrow as we feel most comfortable as we strive to *Live Life as a Prayer*. Yet, to be safe, and to be authentic in our loving and being love, they must be founded in trust.

The kind of love that is trusted, safe and secure. Love without fears. Love with full connection. Love that is *free* to blossom and grow. *Love you can trust.*

Let us agree for the moment *and for the duration of this exploration*, that Love is active, it is a communion, a covenant. And to achieve it requires mutual understanding and trust.

Research professor Dr. Brené Brown has provided us with *The Anatomy of Trust* in which describes "Seven Elements of Trust." Seven elements of being able to be Trusting <u>and Trustworthy</u>. She calls it by the acronym *Braving*. And the words making up the acronym are:

1. Boundaries

2. Reliability

3. Accountability

4. Vault

5. Integrity

6. Non-judgment

7. Generosity

Boundaries. Boundaries are crucial. And, <u>*spoiler-alert*</u>, this is where we go beyond many assumed definitions of the altruistic interpretations of *"unconditional love"* and move towards mutually beneficial *"undoubted love."*

Lack of adequate boundaries can destroy relationships. Lack of clarifying conversations about what each partner's boundaries are can compromise the foundation and set in motion for a relationship to fail. <u>Boundaries</u> <u>are</u> <u>important</u>. Clear understanding of, *and agreements about,* each others boundaries, are necessary in the blueprint of a healthy relationship.

Why?

Because boundaries are the default touchstone to confirm or deny

Trustworthiness in both positive and negative circumstances. For contained in our Boundaries are the things we want, and the things we don't want.

We know these things in our hearts and minds. We cannot assume our partners can read our hearts and minds, nor assume that their boundaries are the same as ours. Boundaries need disclosures and mutual agreements. And, because we are not static creatures, but rather ever evolving in our values, philosophies and spiritualities, these are not one-time conversations established at the beginning of a relationship or as a result of a crisis and never to be spoken of again. *No.*

They need to be updated over time to assure that our partners are aware of subtle and significant shifts in our perceptions, priorities and desires, and that we are aware of theirs. New awarenesses may lead to the need to update our agreements with each other.

Reliability. To build trust in a relationship we need to be mutually reliable. We need to be able to count on each other to do what we say we will do. Consistently.

Accountability. Own your mistakes. We all make them. Apologize and make amends, for in making yourself vulnerable in this way creates avenues for trust. Lying, side-stepping, or blaming someone else for your mistakes creates distrust.

Vault. A vault is a place you can keep what is most valuable to you. So this element of trust equates that you keep the confidences that are told to you. They are placed with you for safe-keeping, not for sharing with anyone other than the person who gave them to you. Most especially is this important in your most personal relationship, your partner, your spouse. They need to be able to trust that you will not gossip about them.

Integrity. Similar to reliability, integrity means our actions align with our words. Practice what we claim are our values, not merely professing them.

Non-judgment. Non-judgment in a trusting relationship allows room for each partner to be able express their feelings or to ask for help without feeling judged.

Now, this can be a tricky one, because it is not an "out" for someone to breach a boundary *or behave without accountability. No.*

A space of non-judgement in a relationship means to not place your values as sacrosanct over someone else's. Non-judgement is accepting someone else's truth even if it is not your own. And - not making them feel guilty about it. Which leads us to the next word in the acronym:

Generosity. Generosity draws upon Rousseauian philosophies of believing in the best intentions of others. If, and more likely, *when,* our partner says or does something that hurts or upsets us, *be generous* with your interpretations of their possible intentions. Do not assume the worst. Do not assume nefarious intentions.

Rather, be open to discovering their *actual* intentions.

Boundaries

Reliability

Accountability

Vault

Integrity

Non-judgment

Generosity

BRAVING.

Braving. For certainly Trusting requires vulnerability and learning the unknown.

As mentioned in the *"Love Enough"* chapter, it is that we collectively do not understand the need to understand each other. And the importance of acting according to what we discover about each other in order to create trust.

We need to trust each other to be able to love each other. We build trust in each other by how we choose to love each other.

This is not a paradox.

Trust is built in large and small moments, large and small actions. So too are feelings of betrayal built in both large and small ways if loving is not attended to thoughtfully.

We need to remember that: Love is not merely a feeling, *Love is an action*.

And <u>loving</u> is not only an ideal: *Loving is a covenant*

We are a people of covenant. To be in covenant is to be in mutual respect and mutual promise. To be in covenant is to hold to our promises even if we have to stretch beyond our comfort zones.

Love is beautiful.

And, loving takes work.

> **Work:** Sustained effort for a purpose to produce a desired result.

To be in covenant also means to forgive each other when we fail, even if we fail a thousand times...
...and we will.

And, even in the wake of failure, in the face of discomfort, unwavering faith can be achieved when partners commit to one another.

> *"To love without knowing how to love <u>wounds</u> the person we love."*

May we learn how to love and be loved in return.

Undoubted Love, *it's a Matter of Trust!*

SACRED SEXUALITY

Let's talk about Sex. Practically speaking, we know that sex is linked to vitality, improved sleep, boosting immunity, lowering blood pressure, decreasing stress levels and even providing pain relief. According to Dr. Mercola in his online aggregated website:

"Regular sex cannot be underestimated as a factor for reducing stress, bolstering self-esteem and fostering feelings of intimacy and bonding between partners." *(Mercola)*

In 2013 Women's Online Health Magazine reported that according to *The Journal of Gerontology*, 732 married couples between the ages of 57-85 were interviewed by researches and the findings were conclusive that the secret to a long and happy marriage is sex. More specifically, engaging regularly in intimacy with their partners.

Nick Drydakis, an economics lecturer at Angila Ruskin University in Cambridge, England, was interviewed by CBSNews.com in 2013 about a study he conducted that concluded that people who were happier, healthier and wealthier were most likely ones who had active sex lives. Drydakis says,

"Sexual activity is a key aspect of personal health

and social welfare that influences individuals across their life span," (*Drydakis*)

Additionally, according to *Psychology Today*, regarding couples specifically in long-term intimate relationships with trusted partners, research consistently shows that the bevy of chemicals released in the brain during sexual activity, including oxytocin, not only increases emotional connection, it also promotes a sense of calm and well-being that can combat patterns of depression and even promote relief of chronic pain.

Yet, with all the practical, biological, chemical, and psychological benefits of sex, it is an area of living that is not given enough contemplative attention, certainly not as it relates to our spirituality. Why?

As touched upon during this book, a human identity that we all cope with is feelings of separateness. We both long for unity and struggle against it in our strivings for self-reliance and individual awakening. Thus the binary tug-of-war that ego places before us. For how can we ever truly achieve awakening to unity as long as we are being stalwarts of autonomy?

As spiritual leaders and ministers, many of us claim as one of our guiding principles the interdependent web of all existence of which we are a part and we look toward direct experiences of transcending mystery and wonder as primary to our primary sources of faith.

Yet, in the area of sexuality many tentatively, some stridently, withdraw from the idea that our sexuality is intrinsically, fundamentally and completely connected to our spiritual life.

Even for those who accredit the quantitative energy exchanges engaging in passion grants us, there remains a dichotomy polarizing the nuanced relationship between sexuality and spirituality. Meaning that somehow, we foster distinctions and gradations and partitions on our sexuality as if it were something separate from us. Thus, separate from our being instead of part of the whole of it.

How did we become estranged from our sexuality? In her book, *Dreaming the Dark: Magic, Sex and Politics* published by Beacon Press in 1998, Starhawk, who is one of the most respected voices in Earth-based spirituality, informs us,

"Sex is an exchange of power in the form of energy that flows between two beings. But the culture of estrangement distorts all power into power-over, into domination. Sexual relations become a field on which questions of power and status are played out. The erotic becomes another arena of domination and submission. Our own sexuality becomes something alien." (*Starhawk*, 137)

Yet, when we reclaim our sexuality as sacred to us, it opens up connections both grounded in our Earthly human experience as well as entangled unity with the ethereal Universal All that we are.

Starhawk continues by saying,

"Sex is energy . . . Understanding that the erotic is energy opens up the potential for an erotic relationship with the earth. We can love nature, not just aesthetically, but carnally . . . that sort of love threatens all the proprieties of estranged culture. Love that mirrors the wildness of nature can move us (to protect Earth) and give us the deep strength we need. That love is connection." *(Starhawk, 143)*

Thomas Moore tells us in *The Soul of Sex: Cultivating Life as an Act of Love* that,

"Sex serves the spiritual life by taking us away from the purely temporal plane for a momentary taste of eternity." *(Moore, 143)*

Whether seeking deeper connective roots with our planet Earth as we embrace this human experience as Holy, or desiring to open up pathways of eternity in union with the Divine from which we come from and are part of, reclaiming our sacred sexuality is essential to *Living Life as a Prayer* and to a holistic, Möbius Life.

Rev. Laura Horton-Ludwig addresses the spiritual aspects of our sexuality in a sermon she gave in Fairfax, Virginia in February 2016 entitled *"Sexuality and Spirituality."* During her service she explores the implication that our spiritual essence and well-being is interconnected with our ability to merge with another human being. She says,

"It's about that energy that moves through the entire universe and breathes through us at every moment. It is called Love and the mystics tell us that it is so powerful that we cannot handle being fully aware of it all times; it is too overwhelming. And yet, we can receive it, filtered through another person. So we can become vessels of divine love for one another. Not just with our hearts, but with these bodies.

And that is why our sexuality is so profoundly connected to our spiritual life. It helps us feel our longing for connection, for love, for union. And if only for a moment know the reality that connection and love and union is what we are, not just what we long for." *(Horton-Ludwig)*

This concept is not new. For millennia humans have been fascinated with the exploration of their sexuality, and the implications of the energetic exchanges that transpire in addition to physical interactions when humans join in sexual experiences. From Magical and Tantric sexual practices to Taoist and Karezza non-orgasmic bonding techniques, investigating towards experiencing the fullness of our sexuality has been of paramount importance to our human experience. As has the movement to place restrictions on our sexuality to limit it to human reproduction, and discounting the emotional, therapeutic, and spiritual benefits of our sexuality.

This is a predominant mechanism for attempting to control the experience of others. The age old falsehood turned myth turned theological teaching of some denominations claiming that "original sin" was one of engaging in sexual intercourse is one such harmful dogma from the patriarchal culture. The misuse or misdirection of Ego analogies in some New Age and Metaphysical doctrines also lead followers to adopt limiting understandings of the importance of wholly incorporating our sexuality into our spirituality. Suggesting that to attain spiritual enlightenment, we must abstain from, or at minimum not be influenced by, human pleasures.

My experience, observations and studies have determined that to attain spiritual enlightenment, spiritual sophistication, spiritual maturity, requires the full acceptance, welcoming and claiming of the human experience. This unequivocally means the integration of our sexuality into our spirituality.

A glance at the etymology of our language, most specifically the roots used in their original meanings, as found online at EtymOnline.com, can help us glean insights to what they can mean for us today. First to better understand the origins, and then to reclaim them for our own theologies.

For instance, when considering our human sexuality, we think naturally of our human desire. The word *"desire"* comes from the latin word *"desidero"* which means to long for. And *"desidero"* comes from *"de+sidus"* to create the phrase *"de sidere"* which means *"from the stars."* Embracing the knowledge that our desires are from the stars, connected to the Universal Oneness, can provide us a place of freedom to embrace our desires as part of the divinity they are. Rather than view our sexuality as a sin, or a vice of the Ego, we can begin to understand that our sexuality is divine, it is sacred, and for us to achieve a fully empowered, fully connected, spiritual life, is to fully experience our sexuality.

Once we do, once we are whole in our spiritual life, we can bring this wholeness to our community. This is a key to Möbius Living and building The Beloved Community. Meaning, the energetic fullness we bring forward into our community as a result of our uninhibited approach to our sacred sexuality creates a positive ripple affect that will strengthen The Beloved Community. We are happier, healthier, body, mind and spirit when we embrace and embody our sacred sexuality. As such, the energy flowing outward from us into our relationships and communities reflects this well-being.

Living Life as a Prayer

LOVE HUMANITY'S CHILDREN WITH YOUR WHOLE HEART

If you have children in your life, do not yell at them, do not hit them, and do not threaten them. If you have children in your life, be kind to them, demonstrate compassion, and protect them from that which can cause them harm. To this end, be fierce about healing your own childhood wounds so that you cease the perpetuation of family cycles of trauma that has been passed on to so many of Humanity's children. Instead, mindfully, carefully, willfully and with absolute understanding and acceptance of your obligation: provide for Humanity's children an inheritance of an intact heart, mind, body and spirit that has been tended to with gentleness and has, as such, generated an environment of a love they can trust in you and, as such, a love they can trust in themselves.

This is where it begins. Yes, sadly, there are real and present dangers that exist at the hand of some criminally insane and morally corrupt strangers and religious extremists. Yet, these are in the minority of those who harm Humanity's children. It is important we educate our children on worldly dangers. Age appropriately, we want to instill in our children their agency over their bodies, their autonomy over their minds, and create environments conducive of freedom of spiritual exploration. We want to actively protect them, and teach them to protect themselves, from predators. We want to create authentic communities within our neighborhoods where all adults are looking out for the best interest of each other's children. Communities that have measures in place to alert residents when dangers exist and systems to protect children therein.

Yet, it is not the strangers nor the extremists in our world that cause the most harm to our children. It is the wounded, broken and unstable families children are forged in that cause the most harm to Humanity's children. Children are a great gift, a magical gift of divine origin. It is our utmost responsibility to care for them and raise them with gentleness. Far to many children are neglected, sexually and physically assaulted, and otherwise abused in their homes. And far too often the abuses are dismissed as irrelevant, covered up as some family's code of silence, or sanctioned by some religious edict. Make no mistake:

- Sexually engaging a child is abuse.
- Hitting a child is abuse.
- Yelling and screaming at a child is abuse.

More than abuse - these are assaults!

If you were to do these acts to an adult without their consent, they would be considered criminal acts. The same should be true for our children. Even more so because adults are supposed to be the protectors of Humanity's children.

With this disclaimer well noted, and the proclamation before us that we are to Love Humanity's Children with our Whole Hearts, we can consider the ways we as parents, as guardians, as families, as communities, can live into this covenant.

At the present time in, it is essential to create communities where children can explore Nature. Where they, too, can develop deep roots as well as be given wings to navigate their journeys. Inculcating love and grace and interconnection in such a way that they know they are part of something bigger than themselves. Yet, giving them space to hear their own purpose calling.

Their own purpose.

Their own calling.

Their own Purpose calling.

Many of on paths of spiritual exploration will readily accept the need to attune to their own highest callings. It is wise to remember that our children, too, have callings. It is our role as parents and guardians to create environments for our children that enables them to most clearly identify their own unique callings.

Often times as parents and guardians, we seek to create better opportunities for our children than we had for ourselves. While this is a laudable intention, it can manifest in harmful ways. Whether from challenged socio-economic backgrounds, or from elite social statuses, parents all too often place their hopes and dreams onto their children in ways that are not in alignment with their child's own innate abilities and deep desires.

Dr. Shefali Tsabary appeared on SuperSoulSunday in August of 2020 to promote her book, *The Awakened*

Family, speaks to this topic. During her interview with Oprah, they discussed the importance of empowering your children by letting go of your expectations of them, and about discerning between "love" and "consciousness." Dr. Shefali Tsabary says, "Love without consciousness becomes need, dependence and control in the name of love." *(Tsabary, 2020)*

A few years earlier in May 2016 during a SuperSoul Session on the Oprah Winfrey network, Dr. Shefali Tsabary decreed, "Our children are not our easels upon which we get to paint the life we never had," she continues. "Our children are not the diamonds and the jewels you get to adorn yourself with to mask your emptiness. And your children are *not* your puppets by which you get to fake an authentic life. Your children do not need that burden on their shoulders." *(Tsabary, 2016)*

While culture endorses the view of bad children whom are challenging vs good children whom we can easily control, it is best to let those ideals go. Such ideals cause feelings of frustration and incompleteness in the parent, and oftentimes are founded in the desire of the parent to give their children a better life than they had. It also causes stress and feelings of upset in the children. Dr. Shefali Tsabary says that only through the liberation of our children can we make sense of what we ourselves went through in our own childhoods. She encourages parents to reflect inward on what their reaction to their children is telling them about their own unresolved childhood needs. Doing so will help us heal any unresolved childhood issues. And doing that will make it possible for us to create environments that are conducive to the well being of the family.

Living Life as a Prayer

The primary goal of parenting children is to create environments for which they can thrive, experience life in healthy ways, learn and grow. As well as creating and modeling a family culture that is loving and nurturing. The rhythms of your family's life will be carried through your child's life into their adulthood, and into their own parenting styles and structures, so it is essential that parents create family cultures consciously. Mindfully doing so, can help identify and root out any negative or unwanted patterns inherited from previous generations, and is an opportunity to bring in new, or retrieve lost, patterns and rituals that will benefit your family, and generations to come.

In the book *Heaven on Earth: a Handbook for Parents of Young Children,* Sharifa Oppenheimer (Oppenheimer, 1) tells us that "young children learn through sensory experience, both energetic and fine movement, and imitating everything they see modeled in their environment."

Oppenheimer sketches out the family culture as a star with these five points:

- discipline: *firm, kind and simple;*
- child's artistic expressions: *various media, music and literature;*
- family work & play: *sharing the workload and playing together;*
- family rhythms: *daily and weekly routines, annual festivals and rituals;*

  AND

- child's play: *imaginative indoor spaces and exploratory outdoor spaces.*

(Oppenheimer, 183)

The ways in which create our family's culture will be inclusive of our personal values and principles. Creating or adopting regular spiritual practices as well as a list of holy days is recommended as they become annual traditions your family can look forward to and plan for. More information about this can be found in the chapter entitled, *"Milestones, Thresholds & Rituals."*

Scheduling time each day and each week to be together as a family, doing activities that benefit the household (such as doing chores together) as well as activities that foster connection (such as family game nights) create a sense of family unity and cultivate love. This sense of unity, and this loving atmosphere, is essential to the body, mind and spirit of the growing child. It is essential, too, for the guardians. Routines and rituals help balance an otherwise chaotic world.

"Parenting is a great adventure" says Julia Cameron in *The Artist's Way for Parents*. "The early years of parenting can be one of the most inspiring chapters of your life, opening you to love and growth you may not have yet experienced. Using these years to tap into your own creativity as well as your child's, you will love and grow together. Awakening your child's sense of curiosity and wonder helps you reawaken your own. Reawakening your own sense of curiosity and wonder helps you awaken your child's. Exercising creativity, alone and together, strengthens the bond between parent and child. Funded by optimism, your child is guided to an expansive and adventurous life." *(Cameron, 5)*

Engaging children in community activities and events regularly creates a sense of rootedness and place in time with the culture of the region you are residing in. It helps children to recognize that they are part of a bigger picture, beyond themselves, beyond their family. Such recognition resonates with and affirms their universal knowing of interconnectedness.

Each family, and every child, is unique. As will be the ways in which we incorporate the above aspects of our family cultures. Whatever age our children are, it is essential we interact with them. Playing age-appropriate games are a wonderful way of teaching skills of boundaries and consequences. Participating in creative activities, even ones we are not particularly skilled at, teaches courage and enhances the child's willingness to try new things. Exploring nature and natural places together connects children and families with our world, and our place on it. Engaging in family rituals and sacred holy days create a sense of unity and purpose.

Children are inherently intuitive, empathic and curious. Their spiritual natures are indistinguishable to them from their human form. Cultures around the world have deified infants and young children. Such as in Bali, Indonesia, where anthropologist Robert Lemelson says, "Before three months, babies are considered holy. Their spirits still belong to the divine. That's why people in Bali always try to treat babies like gods." *(Lemelson)* In Bali the ancient and prevailing custom is that babies are held until they are three to six months old, depending on the community, ensuring an infant's feet do not touch the ground because they are believed to be connected to sacred realms and as such are to be treated with veneration and reverence.

In the Western World, *Indigo, Crystal, Starseed* and *Rainbow* classifications became popularized in the late

20th century as a way of identifying the spiritual, and sometimes perceived supernatural, traits of children. Many present-day religious and spiritual cultures share beliefs that children are reincarnated ancestors or spiritual beings who have chosen to be reborn in human form.

Whatever our beliefs are about our children's origins and purposes, it is our responsibility as parents and guardians to protect them, to nurture and nourish them, and to create homes and environments and communities where they can explore their life's journey in imaginative, creative, artistic and spiritual ways.

Living Life as a Prayer

BORROWED TIME

Life is Change
Time is Precious
and
We are responsible for how we handle both.

This Dance of ours, Life's Journey, consists of Time and the Choices we make. Choosing directions for our Life's course and perpetual migrations to live in to those choices. Some directions are complicated. Some Migrations are short distances. We carry from these our memories and the ramifications of Time and of Choices.

One of my most vivid memories of childhood was on moving day 1976. I was five years old. My sister Audrey was four. We were dressed in similar outfits, as was often the case, and we both had huge – I mean HUGE – lolly pops in our hands. We were walking down the street in Jamaica Plain/ a Boston city neighborhood with our Nana. We were so happy to have such fanciful treats. My baby brother, Charlie, was in his stroller, asleep and in the care of someone else. While my mother packed, my father and others loaded a large truck. We were moving from Boston – where we, my siblings and I, were born, and my father and his whole family lived from the time the first of our ancestors came to America. We were moving to my mother's Canadian homeland: Prince Edward Island.

A typical American life snapshot. A family relocating to a picturesque location. Idyllic to an onlooker, or someone with just the small amount of details I've just described. Yet, what led to that moment in time was not so idyllic.

Jamaica Plain ("JP" as we locals call it) for the past decade or so has been an up and coming, and now sought after, urban residential and business locale. It has evolved in to a truly diverse and dynamic community. Yet, when I was a child, during Boston's attempted early desegregation period of the 70s, it was a dangerous hub of gang activity and racial unrest. Many of those with means to do so, left. Usually the decision to do so quickly following the metaphoric "last straw."

For our family, the final straw in a series of scary moments, was the day the detectives came to search our back yard for stray bullets from a drive by shooting. *Stray Bullets. In Our Back Yard.* As I recounted this story in a sermon for the first time, I felt vivid connection to the overwhelming fear and pain of my parents awakening in me and tears came to my eyes, and to the eyes of those listening. What was once to me a mere story, marking an intersection in my family's lives, transformed and took on profound meaning for me in a way I had never quite felt before.

The complete reality of it finally sinking in then, and again now. For my parents, especially my father, the pain of having to choose to leave what was known was outweighed by the clear and present danger of staying. His priority was his wife and his young family. So, he left behind other family, some very unhappy with his decision. Some even ostracizing him for doing so. And from that moment on, changing the course of all our lives.

Of course I didn't know any of that then. And while my life was carried forward by the choices my parents made to keep us safe. And their decisions stemming from choices others in our community were making to create chaos, I hold only the memory of those giant lollypops. And running gleefully down the sidewalk with my sister and my Nana keeping us in check.

Memories like this point to three Universal Truths: Life is Change; Time is Precious, and; We are responsible for how we handle both. Yes, indeed:

Life is Change

Time is Precious

and

We are responsible for how we handle both.

How effectively we do so (handle both) depends alot on how we perceive things. And what our mode of operation is in life. Möbius Living calls us to be mindful of our moderation of this life. Mary Oliver incites us in her poem entitled *"The Summer Day,"* published in the *House of Light* collection in 1990 by Beacon Press, to question our life's direction by asking the oft quoted words:

"Tell me, what is it you plan to do with your one wild and precious life?" *(Oliver, 60)*

Henry David Thoreau's *Walden*, published in 1854, encourages to:

> "Live in each season as it passes; breathe the air, drink the drink, taste the fruit, and resign yourself to the influence of the earth." *(Thoreau, 23)*

Thoreau suggests for us to resign ourselves to the influence of the earth – for there are certainly ebbs and pulls on us. Yes, choices at hand. How do we choose? He helps us here by offering a measuring tool.

> "The cost of a thing is the amount of what I will call life which is required to be exchanged for it, immediately or in the long run." *(Thoreau, 135)*

Life. Time. How much we spend, *or give up,* on something. What we value. How we assess that value. How we perceive that which is before us. How we perceive our choices and how we perceive the creations we make with our choices. And our choices are important, because we are all on borrowed time.

From the moment we awaken to physical birth on our planet, we begin this journey's end. Moving ever toward our destinies. As we meet challenges and are faced with our own mortalities through *the loss of a loved one* or when we ourselves have be diagnosed with *life-threatening illnesses,* we become increasingly aware *how precious Time is.*

When stress is present, we often become blind to the amount of Time we spend in the details of overcoming obstacles. Dealing with the day-to-day silliness this system of things offers in the way of "organization" dilutes the quality of it. That is, dilutes the quality of our Time.

Living Life as a Prayer

As a society, we treat Time as if we have a surplus attached to a lavish line of credit and syphon it into a plethoric gluttony of distractions. We are either numb to, or feel the pressing weight of, the tedious excess expected of our Time.

> Time, a commodity impossible to trade
>
> for its actual value.
>
> *Time,* a trust fund
>
> we cannot save for a rainy day.
>
> Time, a gift that comes with
>
> freedom of will.
>
> *Time,* gaining equity only in legacy.

How important it is to make every moment count. Not all of us have crystal balls that can tell us exactly when the meter runs out. But we can each be responsible moderators of the Time we know we do have – and that Time is Now.

Every moment alive, we get to choose where our Time reserve goes, how we spend it, *and who we allow to draw from it.* Perhaps our greatest responsibility is truly to be mindful of our Time. And as we craft our practices of Time moderation, *Living Life as a Prayer* becomes the Fine Art of Our Lives. As we use this to build our Beloved Communities, we create a tapestry that enriches our families and follow our dreams.

Within the meter of Borrowed Time we remember:

Life is Change;

Time is Precious,

and;

We are responsible for how we handle both.

Living Life as a Prayer

DEATH CHANGES EVERYTHING

"You, having existed, changed everything.

You, having died, changed everything.

And somehow life moves onward."

None of us can know with any certainty what happens after this human life, or what happens before it, or beyond it. None of us can know with any certainty that there is indeed a meaning to life, to living. Let alone a meaning to death and dying. Yet to create a vision for these things is intuitive to human nature.

For as long as humans have etched into stone and written records onto paper, they have documented beliefs in deities, in afterlives, in supernatural elements and creatures.

Humans, out of hope and fear and curiosity and wonder, have created mystical and mysterious stories naming characters and characteristics of that which they identify as holy and sacred and true.

That which they imagine the holiest of places to be:

Elysium, Heaven, Mag Mell, Nirvana, Shambhala, Shangri-la, the Summerland, Svarga, Tír Tairngire, Valhalla, Vaikuntha.

The Theology of Rev. Twinkle Marie Manning

That which they believe to be lost paradises:

Atlantis, Eden, El Dorado, Lemuria, Mu.

That which they imagine are places of punishment:

Hell, Irkalla, Kur, Naraka, Tartarus, Xibalba.

That which they believe to be otherworldly places:

Annwn, Fairyland, Kunlun, Nysa, Olympus, Zerzura.

And, every imaginable kind of creature, both nobel and nefarious:

Aliens, Angels, Banshees, Centaurs, Cerberuses, Demons, Dopplegangers, Dragons, Elves, Fairies, Ghosts, Gnomes, Goblins, Gods, Goddesses, Griffins, Gargoyles, Leprechauns, Leviathan, Melusine, Mermaids, Minotaurs, Mothmen, Nymphs, Phoenixes, Pixies, Reapers, Shadow People, Shapeshifters, Sirens, Sprites, Sylphs, Unicorns, Valkyries, Vampires, Wendigos, Werewolves, Wraiths.

Many who have had near-death experiences recall firsthand accounts of interactions with mystical peoples, places and things. Others who have come back from death's door report there was nothing to see, that death was nothing more than an off switch. Were these experiences their minds playing tricks on them? Offering up one imaginary scenario or another, confirming or challenging their assumed set belief structures?

Humans can, and have and do often, spend lifetimes

attempting to determine the capital "T" truth of this. Yet, I do not believe, at least at this present moment, that unrequited searching is beneficial to *Living Life as a Prayer*.

While I believe spiritual exploration is vital to a healthy human life, I posit that a life well lived is one that is attuned to the here and now. One that is content with living out this human expression to the fullest possible extent, rather than endless searches for confirmations of the hereafter and exhausting strivings towards so called "enlightenment" or "ascension."

We are in these human forms. Whether we are animist, deist or theist, agnostic or atheist, it is to our benefit to Live Life as a Prayer. And, if it feels right in our hearts to hold beliefs illustrating specific forms of afterlives and mystical places and creatures, then I honor that. More than that, I recommend that you create your spiritual practices around the beliefs you hold dear.

What do I believe happens when we die? My response to that has changed over time. I expect it will continue to change, as my journey is an ever-evolving one.

I write this as a woman who has lost many loved ones to death: most recently one of my children.

Over the years I have called upon my dead loved ones, my brother, my father, my mother, my godfather, my grandparents, my lover. All died, most far too young by our human standards. I've reached out to them mostly when I am in the midst of uncertainty, sometimes merely missing them, or when I experience something I know would bring a smile to their faces.

It brings me comfort to do so. To talk with the "ghost" of them. Likewise with the death of my son. I talk with him in dreams and in daylight, just as I do the others. It does not bring them back, but it keeps them close. Some may say it is only the imprint of their memories - I am OK with that. But to me, in the moments I am connecting with them, if feels real and sacred and true.

I am more a deist than a theist, at present. I find it hard to reconcile the horrific situations of war and disease and domestic and community violence and struggle on Earth with the idea that any loving God/dess is monitoring the situation.

Yet, it is hard to let go of the idea of creation for the wonder and the beauty and the mathematical perfection and the synchronicity of Life is too vast to be anything less than magical.

I am also an animist, for I feel the life in all things. So, logically, if there is energetic forces that the human body cannot see, but we can feel or sense, then it stands to reason, at least to me, that there can be shapes and forms of creatures and places that exist as well. And that brings me comfort.

When someone we love dies, we deserve comfort.

When someone we love dies, *we need comfort.*

We need comfort! And we need to take time to rest. Time to care for our own aching heart. Time to sooth our often racing mind. Time to solace our faith. And, eventually, time to process. Processing in our own time.

May we seek and receive comfort and rest and soothing and solace in the ways most helpful to us.

Living Life as a Prayer

"Our son Riley passed away on September 20th, 2019. He was only 22. He had the brightest smile and the bluest blue eyes. He was so sweet and sensitive. He had such a caring and intuitive heart. A true empath. We are shattered by his death.

We've been told as we awaited his transition, he was surrounded by angels and the spirits of his family who passed before him, grandparents, uncles, ancestors. Some among us believe he now resides with Jesus, or a Heaven of his own choosing. Others of us feel his essence is now energy, with freedom to exist in ways he rarely could while on Earth. Still others feel he will soon reincarnate to greet us once again as a new grandchild.

My brother in-law suggests "the angels some saw were really Valkyries taking this warrior who died in his battle to sit at the side of Odin with his forefather warriors for an eternal feast." I can envision that. For my Riley was as strong as any warrior ever to walk this world or any realm beyond. Yet I also believe that after a while of respite at Odin's banquet table, that Riley would embark on a new mission to bring more light to our world.

I miss him.

I love him.

I want to hug him and hold him.

That's all I can say right now."

~ Marie Porter-Manning
September 27th, 2019

When someone we love dies, there is a void in our life. This void will be filled, so it is crucial that we consciously determine what we wish to fill it with. If unattended to, the cultural defaults we've inherited will take root in the space. Grief is a natural thing when coping with the loss of a loved one. Grief, sadness, even anger, all play a role in navigating through the loss. They are not meant to take up permanent residency. Yet they will if you do not prepare and tend to your grief carefully.

Give yourself adequate space and time and mechanisms to heal. If the death was tragic or traumatic for you, you will need more space, and possibly assistance of a therapist to cope and then heal. I do not necessarily affirm the adage that "time heals all wounds" for death is not something humans have found a way to reverse.

The death of a loved one is a lasting change to our lives. Indeed, the death of a loved one changes everything. But, when tenderly attended to, the pain of the loss can be transformed into something beautiful. Doing so will enhance your life force, and your life's experience. Not attending to your grief, will perpetually deplete your life force, and diminish your life's experience.

Know that while moving forward is necessary, "moving on" is impossible. Our loved-one's death was more than a moment; their life is more than a memory. Their existence is ever-present as they shape our lives even now. Because they have lived, your life changed; because they died, your life changed.

Grief is a spectrum and a collage. It contains all our emotions, sometimes at the same time. And, when we lose many people, the recommendation of "move on" may seem as a sanity-saving measure. I promise you it is not. Moving on is impossible. Moving forward is necessary.

Author, Nora McInerny speaks poignantly and pointedly to this in her much acclaimed TED Talk, *"We Don't 'Move on' from Grief. We Move Forward with It."* In her work she discusses how moving forward, such as falling in love with someone new and wonderful after someone you love dies, can help you realize the enormity of what you lost. She affirms that two parallel plot lines can exist and unfurl at once in your life. New and beautiful things and happy things *and* grief for the former and lost things are not two opposing forces, they are strands to the same thing.

Dianalee Velie, Poet Laurette of Newbury, New Hampshire, in her poem entitled, *"Laughter,"* movingly describes the sensation of joy and laughter the first times it occurs amid deep grief as something, *"alien, at first, a mysterious sound we had forgotten."* Something we can be caught off guard by, even embarrassed about when it bubbles up.

"How can joy be excused when it filters through our gallowed gazes?" she questions, as many of us have questioned while grieving. Yet, it is part of our human nature to experience multiple emotions at once, even ones that seem counter to each other. *(Velie, 18)*

We can experience joy alongside our grief, and do.

Be grateful for any joyful moments and feelings that occur during your times of grief. They will help you stay connected to your human experiences rather than be swept away by your grief. They will contribute to healing your broken heart. Acknowledge, accept and embrace whichever emotions are present for you.

The person you lost to death can, and often will, remain ever-present in your life. The deep grief can transition to less painful emotions such as deep gratitude and abiding love, but this is on your timeline, no one else's.

Some may wish to rush you through your grief, or encourage you to bypass it in some way, or simply to handle your grief in the manner in which they've dealt with theirs. Not only is that not fair, it is not healthy. You are the arbitrator of your own grief. Give yourself permission to feel what you feel, to coddle your pain, to hold it as only you can. Give yourself permission to seek help to navigate your grief in the form of a councilor, a sabbatical, a meditative art therapy program or a positive change in your lifestyle.

And, then, when you are ready: give yourself permission to move forward from deep grief. Give yourself permission to live your life fully, even though your vision for that life now must change because the person you were envisioning on that journey with you has died. Living your life fully, embracing joy, moving forward after loss is *Living Your Life as a Prayer*.

The Triage of Grief

They sat with me for hours in this spot. Sometimes talking. Much of the time just being still, gazing at Autumn's tranquil beauty and listening to the sounds of the Lake.

For some this may look like healing.

I know with experienced certainty it is not.

Not yet.

This, this is the perpetual triage of raw grief.

Keep the body still.

Regulate the breath.

Quiet the mind.

Assess the wound.

Allow tears, laughter or lethargy to come.

Keep in check the anger.

When there is energy, do something useful, purposeful.

Ardently cradle the sorrow when it assails.

Repeat.

~ Marie Porter-Manning
October 14th, 2019

The Dark Season

We are at the threshold of the Seasons,
the doorway to the Year,
when the Veil is thin,
and time passes amorphously.

We turn inward as the Darkness beckons us.
We welcome the warmth of the fire,
contemplating the mysteries of the Unseen.

We honor the soft ache in our hearts
for those we have lost:
the people,
the dreams.

And we rest.
For rest we must, to heal.

This is the cycle of death and rebirth;
release and renewal.

We cherish this time
as the lessons it offers
penetrate our knowing.

May we breathe in wisdom
and breathe out patience.

~ Marie Porter-Manning
October 23rd, 2013

Living Life as a Prayer

RESTORE US TO MEMORY

*When you were born,
you cried;
and the world rejoiced.
Live your life so
that when you die,
the world cries
and you rejoice.*

— Navajo Proverb

Mnemosyne *(Nem-o-scene-y)*, the Greek goddess of Memory, was considered one of the most powerful goddesses of her time. Revered during a time when *Memory* was of the utmost importance.

At a time long before the written word was incorporated into language, it was critical to the well-being of an individual and a society who had to rely solely on the lessons and history passed on in an oral tradition.

Mnemosyne is remembered as being the mother of the nine Muses, each of which represents what could be summed up as the embodiment of the human experience:

- History
- Astronomy
- Epic and Love Poetry
- Tragedy
- Comedy
- Dance
- Music, Songs and Religious Hymns

NINE MUSES

Calliope (epic poetry)

Clio (history)

Euterpe (music, song and lyric poetry)

Erato (love poetry)

Melpomene (tragedy)

Polyhymnia (hymns)

Terpsichore (dance)

Thalia (comedy)

Urania (astronomy)

The memory of Mnemosyne was all inclusive! It was the memory of the rules and energies of the universe, the cycle of life, the people, animals and objects on Earth, the memory of how to live in the world. And the world, beyond.

Mnemosyne's memory served as protection, beacon, and blessing.

Another revered female figure both Saint and Goddess, depending on the source: is *Bhrigid, or* Brigid also closely tied to the arts, poetry and memory. A prayer-poem dedicated to her conveys how important memories were to those of Celtic origins:

> *Brigid of the Mantle, encompass us,*
>
> *Lady of the Lambs, protect us,*
>
> *Keeper of the Hearth, kindle us.*
>
> *Beneath your mantle, gather us,*
>
> *And <u>restore us</u> to Memory.*

Poetic examination of this text indicates the use of "Mantle" associates the theme with the part of our brain that plays a large role in the processing of information, in consciousness, awareness, and memory:s (the cerebral cortex).

We can conclude that not only is this a beseeching of being remembered by the Deity, but also having one's own mind transformed to a renewed condition of health so that the essence of memory is whole.

This kind of desire for memory and remembrance is

echoed through many religious sources. Many believe there is an etheric Keeper of such memories, be it Mnemosyne or Brigid, or St. Peter at the Gates of the Christian Heaven.

At a human level, We are each other's Keepers - of Memories. And, we want to share our memories with others. Along our journeys; in our quiet moments; in our public exchanges; in our pursuit of understanding the world we reside in and our purpose in it. We are affected by each other.

And we want to be remembered as who we know ourselves to be. For being remembered as who we know ourselves to be means being understood. To be understood creates a sense of belonging. Which is an intrinsic human desire, indeed, an intrinsic human need.

Cultures around the world for millennia have left evidence of their desire to preserve Memory. Pictographs and Petroglyphs in Arizona; Hieroglyphics in Egypt; Cuneiform *(Coo nā a-form)* Script throughout Iraq, Iran, Syria, and Turkey. Each provide more than a mere glimpse at primitive civilizations that once existed. Often thought of as the mechanism to disseminate the doctrines of gods *and dogma of humans*, these writings and pictures also give insight as to what once were their daily lives, family shapes and sizes, rituals, cultural norms and power structures.

The art portraying the observations of these ancient people, from documenting celestial representations of the solar cycle to characterizing animals, vegetation, landscapes and waterways of the natural, and supernatural, worlds.

Some of such, very subjective in its observational nature, drawing attention to that which must have held significance to the observer, creating a better understanding between ancient artist and present-day patron.

One such example is of rock art recently found in the ancient Egyptian city of Elkab depicting a herd of elephants - one of the elephants has a little elephant inside of it representing a pregnant female. Seemingly a small distinction, yet apparently a rare way of illustrating a gestating animal.

Carved between 4,000-3,500 B.C.E., this discovery in the Spring of 2017 by an expedition of archeologists led by Yale Professor John Coleman Darnell, *(Elkab Desert Archaeological Survey Project)* was surprising to the archeologists.

For while Ancient Egyptian Hieroglyphics and art have been widely found throughout that region, this discovery unveiled monument size hieroglyphs meant to be seen and read from a great distance.

Compared to a modern-day billboard, the location of these inscriptions show a kind of writing that until recently was believed to be only used by the ruling class at that time *and* used for bureaucratic purposes.

Yet prominently placed where they were on what would have been a route well-traveled by the general public, it indicates that the messages on this "road sign" or "wayside pulpit" were readily accessible to the understanding of more than merely the most privileged of the day.

In archaeological frameworks what this means is that

the clock has been turned back and the point in time they have long-believed the Egyptian writing system *first* became accessible to the general population *is much longer ago.*

And while we do not know the artists and scribes by name, their legacy,

their memory of their time on Earth, lives on, grows and expands though these findings. Informing those who have access to it. Then and Now.

So it is, too, with the memories we are creating today. Individually and Collectively. Our connections with each other matter immensely to our memory system. As do the context and content of the experience from which the memory stems. In her song, *"Love Will Remain,"* Sheryl Crow describes beautifully why it is so important to have shared loving memories. She says:

> *"In the quiet of the deepness of the journey,*
>
> *When the darkness is whole:*
>
> *You are lovely;*
>
> *You are comfort;*
>
> *You're forever!*
>
> *Because I have loved, I am changed;*
>
> *Because I have loved, I can see.*
>
> *Because I have loved, I am changed;*
>
> *Because I am loved, I am free.*
>
> *Where love has been, love will remain."*
>
> *(Crow)*

Love is the greatest and most powerful of experiences and of memories.

Memory. It is not just a recollection of *"What once happened."* Memory has a life of its own. In the current moment. Drawing on past, present and anticipate future to inform it. The best way to preserve Long Term Perpetuation of Memory is to pay attention to it as it is unfolding, the magical and the mundane *moments.*

Scientists tell us memories are encoded most strongly when we are paying attention, when we are alert, when we are deeply engaged and when information is meaningful to us. Protective measures can be put in place to better equip us towards the preservation of memory. For we humans have some obstacles to overcome when it comes to what we could call "memory thieves."

Mental and physical health problems in particular interfere with our ability to pay attention and to recall. Depression. Isolation. Also strip away our mind's ability to hold with accuracy recollection of past memories and encoding of new ones as those who are in depressed and/or isolated states are often focused on past events or future worries and replaying such over and over in their minds and as such they are not entirely present for current moments.

Experts in the memory field have noted that socialization is another contributing factor to whether or not our memories are strong. Studies have shown that people with high levels of social integration have a higher rates of recollection. It is suggested this is because social interaction is akin to mental aerobics, maintaining muscle strength - muscle memory if you will. As such interactive, uplifting conversations are a good workout for our brains. Stretching like learning a new language or skill, is like Yoga for our brains.

And while we are considering exercise, as with the rest of our body that improves its health with physical activity that increases blood flow *including to the brain*. This along with consuming nourish foods aide in the brain's neuroplasticity, which helps us to organize information and be flexible and welcoming of new ideas.

Chronic Stress is a key component to memory loss. Similar to Depression, when we are in Chronic Stress mode, we are not fully present for much of Life's genuine experiences. Chronic Stress keeps our bodies on hyper-alert. Many of us are overloaded with work, personal and family responsibilities, and the inundation of negative media and news, which are responded to with increasingly urgent calls to action - one after the other after the other, addressing multitude of public concerns that we focus on.

Our body's stress response mechanisms are meant to signal our minds to become alert and and our bodies to become activate. This physiological stress-response mechanism is designed to make sure we can survive in a crisis. And then reset. Coming back to a calmer state of Being.

Without extended calm periods, our bodies become flooded with chemicals that result in a loss of brain cells and an inability to form new ones. This affects our ability to retain information. It affects our ability to make good decisions. It affects our quality of life, and the quality of Living we can engage with.

Living Life as a Prayer

With the rampant media informing us daily, even hourly, of each impending crisis, *locally, globally*. With ever-emerging movements tugging on our bodies, minds and spirits to contribute all that we are in gestures of solidarity so that we can make the world new again, one can become exhausted!

I am not suggesting everyone who feels called to justice work set down the mantels of social justice, for that would be blasphemy if ever there was such sacrilege to be named for some of my friends and colleagues who pursue justice-seeking activities as their religion.

But what I am suggesting, what I'm imploring, and what I am asking is for you to *give yourself permission to rest.*

Instead of passing thru Life in a blur of pressings and pressure: find balance. Practice being attentive to Nature, to people, to the changes of the season and of the landscapes and of the sky. Notice the light as it shines through your window each morning, and the stars in the nighttime sky.

Notice each other! Pause, and notice how your lover's eyes light up when you enter a room. Lover's: *Let* your eyes *light up* when your lover enters a room!

Smile! Laugh! Smiles and laughter make memories. So do tears. Take time when they are called for. Let them flow and accept what that moment offers. Embrace this human experience.

Take a vacation to explore something new. Visit neighboring faith once in awhile. Try on a new spiritual practice with others. It is an opportunity to make connections with those who share similar values, hopes and dreams.

Sing! I know for many, I am truly preaching to the choir ;) Yes, sing! And Dance. Move as you are able. Hug each other. Dine together. Make memorable moments - into memories.

Healthy Diet and Exercise; Carefree Socialization; *Loving* Relationships; A Sense of Community and Belonging; Mental and Emotional *Rest*; Spiritual Nourishment. All these contribute to better memory storage. All contribute to better Memory Making and *restore you to memory*.

We can be inspired by memory. Or haunted by it. The parallel of which is to resolve. So that what encompasses you is an authentic memory. May we take lesson from the artists and scribes of old, to observe Nature. Observe yourself in relation to all that is, all that ever was, and all that will be. We can strive to preserve our memory. Or allow it to be erased.

May the memories you most cherish continue to serve you; and may you continue to make good memories together, and hold them close. Remember you belong to each other. And, in the worlds of Linda Koehler Smith, Remember: *Where* ever you are - you are on holy ground; *When* ever you are - you are living in sacred time; *Who* ever you are with - you are in the presence of the divine. So whatever you do keep that in mind. *Keep that in mind*. Remember who you are and live your life in such a way that you will be remembered as who you want to be remembered as.

May Love reside where you are. May you take time to rest. And, may you live your Life so that you rejoice!

Living Life as a Prayer

RECLAIMING MEDITATION:

We are born to this world beautiful and unique.
Over time parts of ourselves are taken away,
Depleting us, making us feel *less than* ourselves.

Some parts we've given away freely
to the aide and comfort and love
of those we wish to share such gifts with.

Other parts of ourselves are taken selfishly by others,
Sometimes forcefully
Sometimes without our consent.

Whether gone by innocence, ignorance or force,
It is important for us to *reclaim* these parts of ourselves.

To restore **us** to our *own* memory;

To our own fullness of Being,

So that we may be equipped
to do the work that is yet to be done.

And to experience Life
in a way that is most meaningful to us.

I invite you to enter into meditation,
With your minds, hearts and hands *ready to receive*.

Let us **retrieve** what is yours!
Hands, either held high,
or holding your heart
And your faces tilted skyward
or Bowed
With Eyes closed.

Breathe
Envision the Circle of the Earth...
...and your place on it.

Envision places you've been, people you've interacted with:
Friends and Foe.
Breathe *and <u>beckon the air to stir as you Will</u>*
from the North,
from the East,
from the South
from the West. *(...breathe)*
Breathe into the Center of yourself. *(...breathe)*

<u>See</u> Yourself in your Mind's Eye
As you reach into your connection to the Earth,
and outward to your connection with the Universe.
hear <u>your own voice</u> say:

I draw back to myself the parts of me
left behind - or taken by others,
For they are mine
and I need them now.

Living Life as a Prayer

From within every place they reside that is not Me
I call these parts of me back
To this time
This place
To me

I take back what is mine
and mine alone

To recharge my Spirit
<u>and</u> my body

To enliven
To strengthen
To awaken
To affirm

To restore to memory
<u>Who</u> I know myself to be
(...breathe)
Return and
Reside with me
To restore and regenerate
So I may stay complete and whole
To charge my actions and my thoughts
To empower my Source, my Soul and my Being
All ways and Always

**May it be known
That I retrieve all that I am
To do all I am meant to.
From this moment on.**
*(...breathe)
In the silence that holds us
In this sanctuary that keeps us
May we breathe in Delight
in this coming home to ourselves.
(...breathe)*

Amen. Amen. Amen.
*(...breathe)
(...breathe)
(...breathe)*

Living Life as a Prayer

HOSPITALITY - A PILLAR OF FAITH

I believe hospitality to be a pillar of Faith. And that radical hospitality enables loving communities to become The Beloved Community. Radical hospitality means demonstrating the courage to try something new to connect with people in meaningful ways. Such radical hospitality was the code of the land in Ancient Ireland,

"O King of stars!

Whether my house be dark or bright,

Never shall it be closed against any one."

(Irish Blessing)

When I opened my spiritual retreat home, I added to that to include, ***"of kind heart"*** because while I believe in acknowledging the connection we share with everyone, I walk closely with those who are of kind hearts. So my radical invitation is to *"all those of kind heart who are seeking shelter, a place of peace, nourishing food, and, most importantly those seeking spiritual sanctuary and beloved community."*

Those who have learned the Gaelic language soon discover that there is no word for "hello." Casual hello does not exist. Instead, those in that culture, using Gaelic, always greet each other with blessing. Every would-be "hello" thus becomes a blessing ritual of encounter.

My friend and colleague, Ian White Maher, whose words I shared early on in this book revealing to us that when we bless someone everything in our life changes. He also talks about our deep need for Empathetic Witness. The kind of seeing and being seen that only happens in the close circle of friendship. Additionally, addressing the topic of loneliness and speaking about prophetic evangelism in a May 2017 podcast, he suggests that evangelism, invitations to community, should never be about converting others, it should always be about letting them know that they are precious to us. He distinguishes between evangelism and growth by stating that,

"Growth is about convincing people to join your group. Evangelism is about trying to change their lives." *(Maher)*

It is important to understand this distinction and that while they may look the same, they fundamentally are different. It is the encounter with spiritual joy that enables us to become conduits for sharing encounters with the divine.

Ian tells us that,

"If your members are having powerful spiritual experiences, if they are being challenged and fed spiritually, they will tell their friends, naturally. Because they are filled with joy."

Being present and active in spiritual evangelism creates connections founded in right relationship and right motivationality. Finding sincere and creative

Living Life as a Prayer

ways to embrace the larger community through radical hospitality draws in those energetically aligned to such invitations. Being clear about the kind of principles and foundational creeds and practices sacrosanct to the kind of spiritual lifestyle envisioned ensures stability within The Beloved Community, even as it is being created.

Acknowledgement, too, of our motives for extending such invitations into The Beloved Community is of utmost importance. Creating a sacred space where those who come, feel the authentic welcome and know they are cherished and wanted, are all keys to creating The Beloved Community.

They are all interconnected and emulated elements of *Living Life as a Prayer*.

The Theology of Rev. Twinkle Marie Manning

COMING HOME
(WATER COMMUNION)

As we continue to turn our attention to the Sacred, may this service become a vessel that holds all that we call Holy. May those who are seeking spiritual sanctuary find solace in such gatherings.

Starhawk's vision of a "Circle of Friends" in her book *Dreaming the Dark* invites us to consider what it means to be in Community. She says:

> "We are all longing to go home to some place we have never been, a place half-remembered and half-envisioned, we can only catch glimpses of from time to time. Community. Somewhere, there are people to whom we can speak with passion without having the words catch in our throats. Somewhere a circle of hands will open to receive us, eyes will light up as we enter, voices will celebrate with us whenever we come into our own power. Community means strength that joins our strength to do the work that needs to be done. Arms to hold us when we falter. A circle of healing. A circle of friends. Someplace where we can be free."
>
> (Starhawk, 92)

Living Life as a Prayer

"*The Winds of Summer*" by Patricia Shuttee offers a beautiful glimpse of what it looks like to return to each other after a time apart. Whether we have gone some place for the summer and are returning to our homes and home congregations. Or, as a way of marking the milestone of summer transitioning into autumn. She writes:

> "*You and I and all of us blew about with the winds of summer.*
>
> *Following the sun in different ways of freedom and play.*
>
> *Finding rest in the cool stillness of shadows, and moving to the slow heat-struck rhythms which turned the long hours of summer light.*
>
> *Now it is time for gathering in. We come together at this time and in this place on the bridge of autumn.*
>
> *Summer is fading backward into memory, and winter waits in snowy brilliance.*
>
> *We meet with eagerness and delight, needing one another for sharing.*
>
> *We have joys and sorrows and hopes to share, questions, things we care about and want to help make better.*
>
> *Things that we would like to understand, ideas waiting to be heard.*
>
> *Today we are together in gladness, once more the special community that we call our church.*
>
> *A community of all ages that sings its songs, tells its thoughts, asks its questions, and searches together with courage and love.*"

(Shuttee)

The Theology of Rev. Twinkle Marie Manning

The Winds of Summer beckon us forward to welcome the incoming of the Season's end. Reminding us that it is Time once again to gather in. Gather in to this place where we know we are welcome, accepted, and where we can be free.

This place where a circle of hands will open to receive us, *and* arms will hold us when we falter. Where we can work together, and explore together. Community, and that which we call Holy.

That which, like water, can have many forms and qualities. It can rain down upon us drenching our spirits with much needed nourishment; refreshing and replenishing that which would otherwise be parched and wanting.

It can, like mist, roll in unexpectedly, surrounding us in mystery and wonder. It can like ice remind us that there is so much more than what meets us at the surface of what we encounter. Encouraging us to look deeper, explore deeper, and live deeper into our faith.

Know that as we gather together, we are mindfully creating space

to hold our most sacred intentions and experiences. And we do so in union with congregations throughout the Nation. It was determined in a vision statement by colleagues that we, "envision a life filled with compassion for all, shared in beloved community, lived in a just and peaceable world."

This vision, and the ideal it conveys, continues to shape a collective vision for many organizations and help professional and lay leaders shape the future of a liberal religious faith tradition.

Living Life as a Prayer

It is something that congregations and congregants, autonomous in their function within both creedless and creedal faiths, can unite in this shared vision of active benevolence and genuine compassion. Whether adhering various denominational doctrines or following paths closely aligned with the natural world, we can claim a vast umbrella of sources to house many paths of religious and spiritual exploration. All come together within the safe harbor our *The Church of Kineo* as we strive to welcome in *radical acceptance* each person on their journey towards home.

We belong together. We belong *to* each other.

We mark this belonging each year when we gather for our adopted homecoming ritual of The Water Communion. The Water Communion has its roots in Unitarian Universalism's 6th source, which is derived from the spiritual teachings of earth-centered traditions which celebrate the sacred circle of life and instruct humans to live in harmony with the rhythms of nature.

Notably, this is one of the places that *The Church of Kineo* aligns with that denomination. More closely though, with the spiritual leaders who actively practice Earth-based, Nature-based and Esoteric rituals and lifestyles.

This Earth Based ritual grew up out of projects created as part of the 1977 UU Women and Religion Resolution which was designed to affirm women's experiences within the organization. Most specifically, *the feminine divine*, goddess tradition and *shared leadership models* that patriarchy had long since driven out of Earth's popular religions.

The original water ceremony entitled: "Coming Home, Like Rivers to the Sea: A Woman's Ritual" was created by Carolyn McDade and Lucile Schuck Longview for the worship service for the November 1980

Women and Religion Continental Convocation in East Lansing, Michigan. Almost two decades later, it was printed for distribution at the 1997 General Assembly of Unitarian Universalists in Phoenix, Arizona. And since that time has morphed into annual ingathering services hosted by interfaith congregations throughout the world. Which was expected and anticipated by its creators as such would be in alignment with the ever-evolving living faith traditions.

With that sentiment in mind, the creators of the Water Communion Ritual said this in their "Sharing of the Waters":

> *"As water changes form and moves in a life-giving cycle,*
>
> *so this water ceremony must move,*
>
> *be in process, change, be in motion.*
>
> *It needs always to be reflective of and integral to*
>
> *the time and place of the people creating it."*
>
> (McDade and Schuck Longview)

Two decades after its original creation, Carolyn and Rosemary and the other women involved with the original ceremony expressed the value of the collaborative process it took to create the service. Their reflections mirror what being in Beloved Community can be for those actively participating in the shaping of such a community. They said,

"Creating that service ... brought us together for many hours of sharing and conversation, analyzing, planning, creating, clarifying. It called us to articulation, to pulling foggy-shaped thoughts into words. We each spoke and listened. We wrote down one another's words. We spoke them back with added meaning. It was a bonding and empowering experience for us, and we commend this sort of experience to you."

As they worked on preparing the service, their awareness increased about Water's presence and deep meaning in our lives. Water became more than simply a metaphor. For it is elemental and primary. It calls forth feelings of awe and reverence.

They blessed the future of the Water Communion and the Sharing of the Waters with the hope that those who drew upon it would reach for the depth and inclusiveness of such symbolism in acknowledgement that we, *"need symbols with enabling power that connect us with what we most deeply value and which empower our expression of this in our lives."*

Here in *The Church of Kineo* we are welcome to be ourselves, offering comfort and strength to one another.

Here, we heal and we hone. To do the work that needs to be done, to Build The Beloved Community. Ever learning, ever growing, meeting challenges, solving problems, gathering together, creating sacred space. Holding our joys, along with our sorrows, lifting each other up, offering blessing, and Loving each other.

Knowing we are part of a larger family in fellowship and sisterhood. Celebrating the sacred Circle of Life. Sometimes blown about with the Winds of Summer. And, always finding our way Home to the Havens of our Congregations and the places and people to whom we belong to. Like the Rivers to the Sea.

May it be so. Blessed Be and Amen.

Living Life as a Prayer

MEDITATION + WATER COMMUNION RITUAL

Imagine this room as a Lake.
Each of us brought here as a drop of rain,
or
through the currents of connecting streams;
weaving and winding through the mountains,
over farmlands, and valleys...

Arriving here together,
intertwined on our journeys and experiences.
Imagine there is a River that flows from this Lake to
a great Ocean of all that is *Living and Loved*.
<u>The Ocean</u> - *Our Source*.
And we - *the <u>Waters of the Rivers Coming Home to Her</u>*.
United
and peaceful
and whole.
If you brought water with you today,
please take the vessel in your hands.
If you did not bring water, please cup your hands
and envision holding beautiful pristine water.

I invite you to Close your eyes for a moment
Just a moment
and breathe. ((breathe))

"May we enter the Holy Quiet:
That place of Being that is within us,
and through us, and beyond us."

The Theology of Rev. Twinkle Marie Manning

Let us bless the water we hold in our hands.
May this water be a symbol of our individual journeys
Even as our communal vessel represents
our covenanted community and all which we call Holy

As we pour our waters <u>into One</u>

May we recognize we <u>Are One</u>...

May we discern the droplets contain

our joys along with our sorrows...

May our sharing of these waters

be in demonstration of our intention

to create throughout the coming year

<u>deeper connections</u> with each other

and <u>spaces so sacred</u>

that they <u>can contain</u>

<u>all our triumphs</u> along with <u>all our fears</u>.

Please come forward if you wish

and pour your water into the vessel.

Feel free to share a word or a sentence about why the source of the water is of special significance to you.

For example:

I share this water from Moosehead Lake
in gratitude for dreams come true.

I share this water from Prince Edward
Island as a symbol of love and hope.

May we be blessed by this sharing
and may we be blessings to each other.

Living Life as a Prayer

GENTLE RIPPLES

(WATER COMMUNION)

Everything we do creates a ripple.

Coretta Scott King said, "The greatness of a community is most accurately measured by the compassionate actions of its members." (Scott King)

Yes, as a people of covenant, there are measurable things that bind us when we gather together. The measurement of compassion can be a touchstone we hold to.

In the envisioning for *Living Life as a Prayer*, and in the founding of the tenets for *The Church of Kineo*, deep contemplation and esoteric assembly went into the idea, ideals and benefits of a compassionate community.

For, as we've explored previously in these principles of *Living Life as a Prayer*, what if hospitality was the pillar of our Faith? If coming together created sanctuary? If sharing Joys and Sorrows was the path to enlightenment? What if our sacred texts were our sermons, poems and songs? If our principles were our doctrines? If our covenant was the Hope that binds us? Indeed, what if compassion presided over our thoughts and our deeds?

The Theology of Rev. Twinkle Marie Manning

In his poem, *"This Sacred Place,"* Rev. Stephen Shick tells us: "This place has been waiting for us, To draw from it a breath of common purpose...To listen to the wisdom of its silence...To fill it with the urgency of new possibilities...To make it sacred by our coming together in compassion." *(Shick)*

Each year at Summertime's end we are beckoned to come together in ritual and in communion – a ceremony that reminds us that we belong together, even as it marks this Holy Season September brings. And, *because* we belong together, we are called to exercise compassion towards each other, and, towards ourselves.

It is the act of compassion that awakens us to bring forth our best gifts to our community. It is the act of self-compassion that emboldens us to be brave, and by 'be brave,' I mean it is self-compassion that allows us to be vulnerable enough to give over our burdens and our sorrows into the tender loving care of our community.

Shared vulnerability, sharing our most joyful experiences, along with our sorrows, this is what builds strength. Strength in our community. Strength in each of us. This strength affirms the depth of compassion that exists here. We gather in to this place where we know we are welcome, accepted, and where we can be free.

This place where our congregation and community will open to receive us, and arms will hold us when we falter. Where we can work together, and explore together. Where we can experience and relate to that which we call Holy. Where we can question answers we've been given that do not resonate.

Living Life as a Prayer

Where we can freely and responsibly search for truth and meaning.

It is in this sacred place that we can see with clarity how every act creates a ripple. Everything we do, even the slightest thing we do, can have a ripple effect and repercussions that emanate. Every word that we speak, every action that we make affects other people, our community and our planet. How important it is that we align our thoughts, words and deeds with compassion, so that the ripples we are bound to create are compassionate ones.

Know that as we gather together, our water ritual serves as a reminder to hold our most sacred intentions of compassionate community in our hearts and at the forefront of our minds.

May this ritual of ingathering remind us and empower us to do the work that needs to be done out in the world, yes, but also, importantly, here in our congregation and communities, and, especially, in our own hearts and minds.

May we cultivate a shared Vision of a life filled with compassion for all, shared in beloved community, and lived in a just and peaceable world. With every compassionate action, we re-commit ourselves to pursuing this vision.

In a world fraught with stress, compassion is the salve that we most need to heal our suffering and free ourselves to be able to embody the kind of tenderness that allows us to naturally act from a caring heart, speaking words that resemble the kindness we wish to exist in our world.

Yes, Compassion is an intrinsic expression of the welcome and acceptance we offer to one another in this sacred place. Compassion is the <u>measure</u> of The Beloved Community. And it is the way we are able to provide solace for the heart that is breaking alongside the heart that is overflowing with joy. Both, and more, reside here simultaneously. It is compassion that allows us to hold both, and all.

Yes, move gently on this earth with compassionate ripples marking your path. For <u>*you*</u> journey with beings, who, just like you, all want to be happy, and welcome and free. Just like you, they all need love, and hope and understanding. Just like you; Just like you; Just like you.

Everything we do creates a ripple. Let our ripples be ones of compassion. May they intertwine and connect with other compassionate ripples.

So that we may create a world of peace and tender affection, beginning - here. With our hands on our heart and Living Life as a Prayer.

Living Life as a Prayer
MEDITATION + WATER COMMUNION RITUAL
Let's create some gentle ripples together.

Today I invite you into ritual, into ceremony,
into communion.

I invite you to bring your gifts, yes,
but also, bring your wounds to heal
and your burdens to share.

Buddhist teacher, Tara Brach, informs us that,

*"Learning to hold our own lives with a gentle
compassion is a key element in all emotional
healing and spiritual awakening."*

With that in mind,

Today we will create a sacred space to allow us to
release that which burdens us, even as we bestow
unto our community our gifts.

Please take a stone from the basket being passed around.

There are many varieties of stones in the basket.

Stones that are jagged, stones that are smooth,
stones that are ugly, stones that are beautiful.

Resembling the multitude of ways our sorrows and
our burdens manifest in our lives:

Jagged ones that cut us, wound us, daily
with their edges;

Smooth ones that we've carried for what
seems like eternity

- they are almost polished by the weathering
of time,

and the worrying of our attention;

Ugly ones for the fears and feelings they bring up in us

- ours and others;

Beautiful ones that hide their painfully raw <u>interiors</u>,

even as the burdens we all too often carry are hidden by

our beautiful smiles

so as not to place the weight of them

on the people we interact with,

the people we love.

Please take a stone that resonates with you.

Take it knowing you will release it.

Hold it in your hands,

name something your body, heart, mind and spirit, would benefit from your letting go of

and let the stone absorb that

which you most want to release,

or if not release,

if that seems too impossible a task,

because sometimes there are things that exist in our lives

that will always exist,

or exist for a time to come,

Living Life as a Prayer

even so, hold that stone
and let it absorb the parts of your burden
you are willing to release
into this community that loves you.

Hold it, hold it and release your burden.

Say it in silence, for there is power in its
acknowledgement.
or, Speak it aloud if you wish,
for there is great power in words.

Let us bless the stone we hold in our hands.

*May we imbue this stone with that which has been
our burden to carry alone.*

**Now, as the basket comes back around again,
place that stone back into it, along with your
burden - <u>to release or to share.</u>**

*May we release it to that which we call Holy,
and into the gentle care
of this community's loving embrace.*

**(Leader adds the stones to the primary water
bowl and assistant gathers participants stones
to place in basket, then water)**

(Then continues...to water ritual)):

If you brought water with you today, please take the
vessel in your hands.

If you did not bring water, please cup your hands and envision holding beautiful pristine water.

I invite you to Close your eyes for a moment
Just a moment
and breathe. ((breathe))

"May we enter the Holy Quiet:
That place of Being that is within us,
and through us, and beyond us."

Let us bless the water we hold in our hands.

"May this water be a symbol of our individual journeys, our strengths and our prayers.

Even as our communal vessel represents our covenanted community and all which we call Holy

As we pour our waters <u>into One</u>

May we recognize we <u>Are One</u>...

May the water wash over the burdens and sorrows we have also placed into the care of this community

*May we discern the ripples we create together with
the stones,
the water,
we combine our joys along
and wash over our sorrows...*

*May our sharing of these waters
be in demonstration of our loving intention
to create throughout the coming year*

Living Life as a Prayer

<u>deeper more compassion connections</u>
with each other
that we are able to hold
<u>spaces so sacred</u>
that they <u>can contain</u>

<u>all our triumphs</u> along with <u>all our fears</u>.

**Please come forward if you wish
and pour your water into the vessel.**

Feel free to share a word or a sentence about why the source of the water is of special significance to you.

Know that each drop and every word creates a ripple that can contribute to the healing of sorrows, and the building of compassion, yes the building of This Beloved Community.

For example:

*I share this water from Moosehead Lake
in gratitude for dreams come true.*

*I share this water from Prince Edward
Island as a symbol of love and hope.*

May we be blessed by this sharing

and may we be blessings to each other.

May our church community be

United

and peaceful

and whole.

Amen.

The Theology of Rev. Twinkle Marie Manning

Above pictured: Rockwood, Maine, USA

Above pictured: Argyle Shore, PEI, Canada

ON ART AND CENTERING

Years ago I was a member of the PEI Potter's Guild. At that time I was raising three young children and one of my few creative outlets was the *Guild's studio*. It was an old gate house in Victoria Park. Near the water and surrounded by sprawling green landscape. Each Guild member was given a key and able to come and go as she pleased. There were classes we could take *and give.* And space *galore* to create. I had the blessing of an eccentric teacher (Carl Phyllis, Master Potter and Metalworks Sculptor) who held a strong belief that *"life is art,* and *art is life."*

From this place of expansive thinking, it was possible for him to grant his students a lot of freedom, a lot of individualized coaching. Carl understood I was not in his class to cultivate the skill required to earn a living with this craft. No, I was there to channel my energies into the clay. To have it be both *the source of my creation,* and *the inspiration for it.* The place where in solitude, or in community, I could work through the struggles of my human conditioning as I worked through the clay. Molding it, as I alone could mold myself, birthing my emerging creations of clay and of self into my new identity.

In that space of identity-crafting, my teacher's greatest gift to me was a simple four-word comment. Sure, he taught me to center, to fire, to glaze, and all other necessary potter's techniques. He taught me the fun and artistry of a home-made Raku container and the metallic luster that could be achieved by adding autumn leaves or spring flowers. He taught me the craft and gave me the freedom to explore on my own. And, one day when I felt for sure I had just thrown the perfect pot, it caved in on one side -just as he was walking by. Without skipping a beat he said with enthusiasm,

"Ah, now it's art." *(Phyllis)*

And my world shifted. And, I knew for certain as with the lessons of Borrowed Time: *Life is Change; Time is Precious*, and we are responsible for how we handle both. As I think back to those days I realize that was likely one of the first affirmations I received about this emerging concept of Möbius Living. It begins with embracing the Möbius of Life.

A squished up would be bowl of clay... and four simple words issued at lightening speed:

"Ah, now it's art." *(Phyllis)*

Those words have stuck with me over the years, in all aspects of life. Their implications enormous. Our scars, whether physical, mental, emotional or spiritual, are what make us unique works of art, rather than cookie-cutter replicas of what a human "should" be. They shape us, yet we can also shape how they impact us. Perhaps not right away when the wound is raw, but once the initial trauma has passed. If we allow it to heal, neither picking at the scab nor hiding it from oxygen, we may be surprised at what beauty can be discovered.

Living Life as a Prayer

The bowl I was creating on that wheel so long ago, it could not hold soup as I once intended, I could have tossed it aside declaring it ruined forever. Instead, I heeded the wisdom from my teacher and it now holds so much more beauty, and so much more meaning to me, than it could have as a mere bowl.

Each of us as we hold the (emotional/mental) scars of the awful things done to us - and the awful things we have done to others, can choose to keep the wounds open, picking at them, allowing them to eat away at us, forging the scar tissue to build so thick in attempts to block out the memory of the trauma. Or we can choose to open the window on them, give them fresh air, acknowledge their existence, allow them to truly heal, and embrace what we discover.

Another thought, again with clay metaphor in mind, is that if we find that there is a part of us that is completely broken from a trauma, there is a special pottery art for that too: Kintsugi. With Kintsugi we do not attempt to disguise the flaw, rather assemble it back together and glaze it revealing the broken parts as part of the history of the bowl. It does not look as it originally did, but it honors what it is now. Always, it is amazingly beautiful.

Life, like the creation of pottery, is about *balancing* and *centering*. For those who've sat at – or watched a potter at – the potter's wheel, you can visualize the process. The mound of clay centered on the wheel, spinning in the guiding embrace of the potter's hands. The centering is crucial to the integrity of the pot.

Mystic, Poet and Master Potter M.C. Richards writes in her book published in 1964 by Wesleyan University

Press entitled, *Centering: in Pottery, Poetry, and the Person.*

"Centering is an act of bringing in, not leaving out. It is brought about not by force but by coordinations. It is difficult if not impossible for a potter to force his clay into center simply by exerted pressure. In order to take its new shape, the clay has to move." (*Richards*, 35)

Such as it is with life. We can attempt to force it in the direction of our choosing, but how much more effective it is when we encourage it with gentle nudges to bring it into center.

Richards continues by saying,

"Because the wheel is center-oriented, the ball of clay will take a centered position naturally if we can create the necessary support and influence." (*Richards*, 35)

I believe So too with life! It is center-oriented. A supportive force, designed to bring us naturally into alignment. The catch? It requires our active participation. In return, it gives us the needed gravitational pull to center. It does not require us to reject any part of our selves. Yet is does demand we have a clear center to orient us. *With that in balance, we can be* confident that we can align all parts as we hold close to our center with seemingly effortless grace.

Each year I lead retreats that revisit the themes of Anne Morrow Lindbergh's 1955 classic book, *Gift from the Sea.* In her reflections on self-realization and adventures in stillness on her Island retreat, she finds herself fascinated with the complex simplicity of the Moon shell. Its smooth circles winding inward to the tiny core that was once home to a snail. Reminding her to wind inward as well. To focus, *in solitude,* on her center. Morrow reflects that the answer to the fragmented lives we have created for ourselves is to achieve stillness. Still as the axis of a wheel in the midst of all our activities. Literally and metaphorically. Centered. That this is the salvation of the self, of the family, of society, and most likely even of our civilization. With such an overwhelming amount of choices in an already overwhelmingly busy life, she says unfortunately and to our detriment,

"We usually select the known, seldom the strange. We tend not to choose the unknown which might be a shock or a disappointment or simply a little difficult to cope with. And yet it is the unknown with all its disappointments and surprises that is the most enriching." *(Lindbergh,* 119)

Yes, here is the fine art of our lives, the centrifugal force crucial in Möbius Living. Risking disappointment, risking failure, risking Love. Because when we do, we give opportunity for Beauty to arise from such risks. We acknowledge our connection to all that is, and release limitations on the outcomes. We open to it, by bringing our best most creative and mindful knowings and practices to it.

Canada's own Lucy Maude Montgomery tells us:

"It's not what the world holds for you. It's what you bring to it." *(Montgomery, 51)*

When we are walking the path we design for ourselves, it can feel almost entirely singular in nature. We know we live in a world of interconnectedness; that our lives intersect with others *and theirs with ours.* We are aware of the "coincidences" that lead us to each given circumstance. But we may view our own journeys, our moments *and theirs*, as linear: progressing and regressing, but single lines nonetheless.

Viewed from a distance, from a bird's-eye view, our lives begin to take on a multi-faceted landscape. The intersections, excursions and milestones piece together to become a vivid tapestry – each one unique. The tiny quiet road we began on. The highway we rallied for space intermingling with others. The foot paths we carved out as we take steps on virgin land. The bridges we crossed. The roadblocks we found our way around. The serene locations that we return to over and over when we need to quiet our minds. The lakes and ponds we created with our tears of sadness and of joy. The fields that have grown – large and small – as we planted seeds of inspiration in ourselves *and* in others. All of these come together to form the fine art of our lives.

All of these we bring forward into the creation of The Beloved Community. The parts we bring as individuals combine with those we meet along our journeys to create a gallery of magnificence.

As we go out into the world,

May we dedicate some time to stillness, and to solitude;

Time to singing and time to dancing.

May we create peace in our relationships,

Love in our hearts; hospitality in our Actions.

May our paths be blessed with kindness and compassion;

And may we be an inspiration to the ever awakening Spirit in all we meet.

Amen and Blessed Be.

SACRED SERVICE

Awhile ago I was asked to craft a sermon supporting social justice work. "Sacred Service" was my response to how one can answer the call to social activism with one's spiritual journey. But it is by no means advocating for or against, for *The Church of Kineo* is clear in the separation of church and state. That said, there is instruction found even as far back as Biblical times, stressing the importance of calling truth to power and speaking out about injustices one sees. Isaiah 58 says, in part, "Shout it aloud, do not hold back. Raise your voice like a trumpet." *(Isaiah 58)*

Some among us say that social activism is in itself a spiritual practice. Others say social activism blends with our spirituality, merged in a way that it is impossible to separate both from the whole of a spiritual practice. Still others believe their social activism and their spirituality are separate, distinct even if aligned, and that it is their deeply held spiritual beliefs that calls them to be social activist. That social activism is the byproduct and companion of spiritual activism.

Yes, our feelings and beliefs about social activism can be as diverse as our feelings and beliefs about spirituality, and about where we draw our sources of faith, about how we practice our faith. Social activism/ Spiritual activism. Sometimes the threads connecting these are bold and clear, and it is easy to distinguish the catalyst that brings one's spiritual paths to answer the call of social activism.

Other times the onlooker may not see the gossamer-like fiber that connects our spiritual experience, that motivates us to respond to meet the needs we see present with practices of social activism.

At *The Church of Kineo,* like many of our liberal religious denominational counterparts, we draw our faith, in all or in part, from a variety of sources, including wisdom from other religions and spiritual paths, teachings of spiritual leaders, as well as our direct experiences with that which we uniquely identify as Holy. As a result, each of us is here today because our unique spiritual journeys led us to this place. Many of us have the desire to explore the transcending mysteries of life and of living.

Transcendentalism has grow up from within the hearts of many. And around the world we are also learning and teaching Analytical, Ethical, Environmental, Technological, Leadership, Dialectic, Cognitive, and Metaphysical philosophies ancient and newly discovered or formed.

From within these vast religious explorations our faith can be as narrow or as broad as feels right for each of us. *What resonates most for us.* Yet in all of this, the many places we individually and collectively draw our faith from, we can ask:

What *is* Spirituality?

Spiritual teacher and author of *Invisible Warfare,* Mona Miller sums it up with two indicators: She says, "all spirituality no matter what the religion is Truth and Love."

Truth and Love. Can it really be that simple? Should it be that simple?

Indeed, in a world as complex as ours...*Should it be that simple?* And, what is Truth? What is Love? How do they connect with our Spirituality?

We can discern "Truth" as being that which cannot be denied, that which our experience confirms, or that which *brings understanding to* our experiences.

Persian poet and scholar, Rūmī informs us that *"Love is the bridge between you and everything."* (Rūmī)

"**Love** is the bridge between you and everything."

And this love, this truth, our spirituality can be emulated through our social activism if we feel it is part of our call in *Living Life as a Prayer*.

Many liberal congregations frequently recite, or even adopt as part of their covenants), the following affirmation:

"Love is our doctrine, the quest for truth is our sacrament, and service is our prayer."

Rev. Peter Morales, a liberal religious minister, says: *"If prayer is the word we use to describe connecting to what is sacred, I think service may be the best form of prayer. And if the purpose of a spiritual practice is spiritual growth, service is a powerful spiritual discipline. I have seen again and again how service transforms people. No one who commits herself to service remains unchanged by the experience. When* we serve we become more compassionate, more sensitive, more understanding, and more aware. We are reminded of how precious and fragile life is. We experience our vulnerability and our deep need for one another. When we serve we experience what love can do." (Morales)

This idea beckons us to consider that to us, as people with all our wildly diverse representations of spiritual practices, Service can be one's Prayer. Said another way, specifically with the intent behind Rev. Morales's definition of "service": *Social Activism* can be one's prayer.

But what calls us toward Social Activism? How do our choices in how and where we serve others meet us on our spiritual journeys? How do we even begin to choose how to serve in such a way? And, who to serve? And, why?

Seane Corn, renown Vinyasa Flow Yoga Teacher and Spiritual Activist,

begins her new memoir *Revolution of the Soul*, by saying: "*My first lessons in spirituality and yoga had nothing to do with a mat, but everything to do with waking up.*" (Corn)

She had discovered, while looking for some unnamed external solutions to what met her on her life's journey, that it was an awakening awareness

within and around her that stoked the embers of her spirituality. And in ways that were a surprise to her.

In a recent interview on *"Sounds True,"* in responding to what was one of the most meaningful discoveries on her spiritual journey, Seane discussed with interviewer Tami Simon, the concept "Your Pain is your Purpose." (28 minute mark of video) What does that mean? "Your Pain is Your Purpose"? In once sense your pain indicates what needs your attention. What needs your care. What needs healing. It also points to what you have direct experience with, and as such gives you connection with others who have experienced similar. Seane explains that:

"The very thing that brings you to your knees The very place that your own journey leads you. For self love, self compassion and empathy, is the very place from which you will be most skilled to be of service." (Corn)

In her journey, because of her personal experiences, the space Seane feels most equipped to hold space for and with is children who have been sexually exploited. Because while she cannot understand exactly what anyone else has gone through as everyone's experience on the spectrum of sexual abuse is their own, but she understands association, she understands betrayal, and the shutdown that can come with that kind of betrayal.

Seane speaks of her ability to not feel pity or sympathy for those she serves as those kinds of feelings are hierarchical because that puts her above them, but rather to feel empathy and so it is not one sided, and because of that they can create a deeper more equal connection with each other.

In relating this to our choices of social activism I would posit that much of the time when we are drawn to serve, we are drawn so out of a reflection of our own pain, and whether in empathy or sympathy we recognize the pain in others and want to help.

Sometimes our pain is so poignant that the place we choose to serve is in direct relation to the source of our own pain. Sometimes we choose to serve in a capacity that is completely separate from the pain we experience in our own lives. But we choose to serve with the innate, if not conscious, understanding that when anyone's pain lessens, when anyone's pain is healed, the world becomes less painful for everyone. Us included.

This is the essence of the respect, the understanding and appreciation of the interdependent web of all existence of which we are a part that compels many in liberal religious faith traditions feel called to seek "social justice" and be active in political campaigns that align with their belief systems. Does this mean we all have to be social activists?

If so, how do we choose which call to answer.

If not, if we don't have to be social activists, and free will tells us we can certainly choose not to, how can we reconcile that choice with the very active members of our community who are social activists? Or with our own congregations when there is a majority or a divide over which social issues to lift up and support when it means that other also important causes will have to be set aside or not given as much attention?

Consider, the components of a healthy spiritual life:

- Acceptance & Discernment
- Appreciation & Integrity
- Compassion & Empathy

Living Life as a Prayer

- Humility & Love

- Kindness & Generosity

- And Service.

Acceptance of what our journey's have been, and where we are now. Discernment about the choices we made to get here vs what was out of our control. Appreciation for the gifts that life has given us, and live our lives with integrity. Be compassionate and have empathy for others. As we know not what the fullness of their journeys have been.

Cultivate humility, admit when we are wrong and correct our course. Embody love. Act in kindness and in generosity to the extent we are able. And find ways to serve if, and in ways, you feel called to.

For some of us this service will be social activism, for others it will be familial attentiveness, or the work we choose to do for a living. Whether we are creating or volunteering in a movement locally or globally to heal some of the world's many injustices. Or, attending to our family's needs: *care of our young children, or ailing parent or spouse.* Or, working as a nurse, a social worker, or a teacher. Or, leading a book group, knitting group, choir, or drum circle.

When we are called to serve, if we create a spiritual practice that serves us well, a spiritual practice that enhances our Quality of Life, our sense of meaning and purpose become clear and our ability to serve others is strengthened. More than that, when our spiritual practice is strong, our service is founded in Truth and Love which will sustain our service.

Without these, our service, and our spiritual journeys may be weakened by the pressures of Life. And when that happens, our ability to serve is also weakened.

A good question to ask ourselves is: How does our inner work, our spiritual work, inform what we need to do in the world?

Is your social activism motivated by a need to feel good about yourself or is it a deep desire to help people? It can, and often is both, yet it is important to name that this duality exists within the work of social activism, and can be balanced, indeed must be aligned with *if there is to be balance,* with one's spiritual practice.

Without such balance our social activism can show up in forms of dominance and savior complex which can perpetuate the power dynamics that create separation and contribute to the very issues that are of most concern in our communities and in our world.

A caution is to not let our social activism be a bypass to our spiritual journey! To dissociate from our own pain. To suppress our own emotions. To ignore signs of Spiritual Atrophy, helps mo one. Be mindful about cultivating a spiritual practice that not only brings you joy, but also serves as a mechanism for you to process your fear and your anger.

Create a spiritual practice that can be a container to hold your tears of sorrow transforming them into the kind of spiritual essence that waters and nourishes the seeds of growth within your own heart and mind so that you are prepared to answer the call to serve others.

Living Life as a Prayer

For many this nourishment is found in Stillness, in Nature, in Ritual. For others it is found in Movement and Dance, Sound and Music.

Whatever calls your Spirit to Life, serve it that. So that *that* which calls upon your Spirit to serve, can be served in Sacred Service, and in emulation of *Living Life as a Prayer*. This is how one answers the call to social activism with one's spiritual journey.

So, does our spiritual journey always intersect with social activism? Contrary to popular opinion among some our liberal religious faith traditions: *No*.

But when it does, individually and as a congregation to ensure our social activism lifts up our community even as it breathes new life into our congregations and revitalizes our members by having our social activism come from a place that is grounded in our spiritual practices of *Living Life as a Prayer*, grounded in Truth and Love: Our Service is Sacred. And we are both a blessing to the world and blessed because of it.

As Rev. Peter Morales has said: *"When we serve we become more compassionate, more sensitive, more understanding, and more aware. When we serve we experience what love can do."* (Morales)

Together, let us live into our individual calls to serve in ways that resonate with our hearts, minds, spirits, and in doing so, may we experience (and demonstrate) what love can do!

May your journeys be blessed. Amen & Blessed Be.

*Note: The Chapter entitled *Be Like The Trees* offers additional insights regarding Sacred Service.

PRELUDE TO BE LIKE THE TREES

First Frost, Excerpts
by Sarah Addison Allen

"The day the (magic) tree bloomed *in the fall*, when its white apple blossoms fell and covered the ground like snow, it was tradition for the Waverleys to gather in the garden like survivors of some great catastrophe, hugging one another, laughing as they touched faces and arms, making sure they were all okay, grateful to have gotten through it."

"A breeze flew through, picking up some leaves and swirling them around, the sound like fluttering pages in a quiet library."

The town, their home - a painted picture:

"It looked like the world was covered in a cobbler crust of brown sugar and cinnamon."

The Waverley house
was filled with food...
"Loaves of fig and pepper bread, of course.

But there was also lasagna cooked in miniature pumpkins, and pumpkin-seed brittle. Roasted red pepper soup, and spiced caramel potato cakes.

Corn muffins and brown sugar popcorn balls and a dozen cupcakes, each with a different frosting,

because what was **First Frost** *without frosting?*

Pear beer and clove ginger ale in dark bottles sat in the icy beverage tub.

They ate well into the afternoon, and the more they ate, the more food there seemed to be.

Pretzel buns and cranberry cheese and walnuts appearing, just when they thought they'd tasted everything."

"The scent spread through the house like a long, soft blanket, settling over everything, calming all worries."

First Frost always marked the milestone that released the Waverleys from the summer's calamities, catastrophes, and compulsivities.

First Frost tamed the whims of their mischievous apple tree.

(And she knew, *Oh She Knew*, as she knew every First Frost):

"She couldn't change who she was,

and she no longer wanted to, *even if she could*.

She knew that **who you are** is a stone **(Seed) set deep inside you.**

You can spend all your life trying to dig that stone **(Seed)** out,

or

you can build around it."

(Nurture it,)

(And ***allow yourself to grow***.)

BE LIKE THE TREES

Sometimes the sermon that you have taken the time to prepare and expect to deliver turns out, as a result of changing circumstances, to not be the sermon that is needed on a given Sunday. And was the case on the Sunday I was to deliver *Be Like the Trees* for the first time.

It had been a difficult week for so many. Those affected by the hurricanes and fires of the last month. Those affected by the violence in Las Vegas that week. When tragedy strikes.... No – *tragedy* is the hurricanes, the earthquake, the fires. Tragedies are the things out of our hands; out of our human capacity to control. Tragedies are the things Mother Nature delivers upon us. But hers is without malice or intention to harm.

> When the wind blows it does not mean topple the butterflies;
>
> Rain does not seek to immobilize the bees.
>
> Hurricanes are not on a mission to take human lives.
>
> And so when they do – it is a tragedy.

Horrific acts of human perpetrated violence...That requires another word – a word that remains elusive, yet describes in full the intention behind the act and the pain it causes. And the pain it causes needs to be acknowledged and calls for the space for that acknowledgement to exist in sacredness: to comfort each other and for healing to take place even though in the moment it occurs, and the moments immediately after, we don't know how it will.

"The Serenity Prayer," originally written by American Theologian Reinhold Niebuhr, modified over time and popularized by 12-step programs, speaks to this need:

"God grant us the serenity
to accept the things we cannot change;
courage to change the things we can;
and wisdom to know the difference."

(Niebuhr)

ORIGINAL SERENITY PRAYER

"God, give us courage to change what must be altered, serenity to accept what cannot be helped, and the insight to know the one from the other."

Reinhold Niebuhr, 1933

The Theology of Rev. Twinkle Marie Manning

This sermon was crafted to speak primarily about trees. But I will also be speaking about grief. About the magic of our human existence. And, about what happens next. What happens – – – Afterward. And also about how we can prepare in advance for the Afterward.

In the words of Saint Francis of Assisi: *"God, make me an instrument of thy peace! That where there is hatred, I may bring love."* Natalie Goldberg in her book *Writing Down the Bones* says: *"They move with grace in and out of many worlds."* (Goldberg)

She is talking specifically about writers, and in a larger way about artists. I feel it applies to all of us who are weaving our way through life with mindfulness. Certainly when seeking to answer our inspirational callings, yet perhaps never more necessarily so than when dealing with times of grief and anger and frustration and fear.

There is little doubt that many worlds are contained in this one consciousness, in this present existence. Both seen and unseen, as often the worlds that exist are beneath the ones that are apparent. The world within our heart that draws us together in times of joy and in times of sorrow. The world within our mind that reasons right from wrong, and strategizes how to deal with either. The world we walk on, our Earth, filled with so much beauty, creative and destructive in its power. Even as we humans can choose to be creative and destructive in our power.

Seemingly contrasting, yet it is the very nature of our lives to discern how to navigate such worlds. How to marry them with each other, and with the worlds contained, and carried, by those we share our lives with. How we process and move forward in the wake of tragedy can be either destructive or creative use of our power individually and collectively. The *Afterward* is a place we all must travel to on our paths towards wholeness and healing.

The Afterward

The Afterward comes at so many times and in so many ways.

I urge you to walk in to the Afterward

Then stop.

Face the Afterward.

Feel the confusion.

Experience the pain, the turmoil and grief.

Consume the uncertainty until you extinguish it.

It may take awhile.

It may happen in an instant.

That's the magic of The Afterward.

Take every ounce of the Afterward that you can grasp.

Gather it up.

Not in a tight unrecognizable way

Rather, loosely – like picking wild flowers from a field.

Reap it.

Thresh it.

Hold it.

Then let it go.

You see,
You need to go into the Afterward.
It is sometimes necessary to stay there for a time.
Stunned by loss and disbelief
Sudden as it is or may be
Emotions rise.
Deal with the distress.
Go inward.
Find your peace;
Find it; hold it *and let it hold you.*
Seek it more deeply
should it be unclear.
Open your hand for help
And know that help is near.
Take comfort when it comes.
And remember:
The Afterward is not meant to be permanent.
Accept that there is more than the Afterward.
There is the Next.
There is Life.
*There is **Now**.*

Jane Roberts tells us: *"You are so part of the world that your slightest action contributes to its reality. Your breath changes the atmosphere. Your encounters with others alter the fabrics of their lives, and the lives of those who come in contact with them." (Roberts)*

Living Life as a Prayer

And so when tragedy strikes, even when we seem removed from it, we feel it nonetheless. We feel the loss, the fear, the anguish, because we are part of each other. And because of this, we are called to serve. Serve each other and serve the world. With our roots holding us close and our wings setting us free.

Yes, in this way we can *Be Like the Trees*. Deep roots. Inner strength. Radiant exterior. Stretching high. Flexible where you stand. Letting go when it's time. Standing tall 'til the end of your days. Breathing and transforming the environment. Offering shelter and comfort and beauty to all who are so fortunate to be in your presence.

Be like the trees, even while pushed and pulled by storms, yet ever aware of our place in time.

When I first wrote *Be Like the Trees* we were in Autumntime in Maine. The season that resonates all senses with its transition. As leaves change color, grass turns from green to brown, crops complete their cycles and temperatures modulate from the warmth of summer to the cold of winter *(here in Maine sometimes in a single day!)* but ever inching in synchronicity with the darkening reflected in the shortened days.

Be like the trees and live each season as it passes. Be still enough to hear your Call to service. Be strong enough to act on it.

What's Your Tree?

In 1997 Julia Butterfly Hill found her tree. Literally. Her tree was named *"Luna,"* a 200 foot tall ancient redwood that was slated to be cut down. Julia climbed up her tree and stayed there for more than 2 years.

She refused to come down until Luna was permanently protected.

She stayed atop Luna withstanding gale force El Niño winds and in the face of death threats by the lumber company. She lived on a tiny platform in Luna's branches for 738 days. Eventually, Julia and those who supported her successfully negotiated to save Luna and a 3 acre buffer zone around the tree. Afterwards she coined the phrase, "What's Your Tree?"

What do you care about so much that you are willing to dedicate years of your life, weather the harshest of storms and possibly even face death to fulfill the purpose of? Julia's tree was Luna, and Luna's family: the Redwood Forest.

Julia's foundation continues to protect the environment in many ways, as well as offers tools to support those who wish to follow their own heart's calling. Yes, in the area of environmental renewal, peace, justice, and also in spiritual fulfillment.

What's Your Tree as a Movement was originally developed for people who were inspired by Julia's story, but it reaches far beyond her "fans." A wide range of people with a diversity of backgrounds participate in What's Your Tree:

- People who want a deeper sense of purpose and stronger focus for their lives.

- People who want to make a difference in their community or in the world but aren't quite sure where to start.

- People who have been making a difference for a long time and are burnt out, overwhelmed or who may be losing their passion.

- People who know that their impact will be multiplied exponentially (and they will have a lot more fun) if they are in a community of like-minded people.

Sound Familiar? What's Your Tree? What purpose are you willing to use your life to fulfill? What's *Our* Tree? It has been said that the purpose of a liberal religious church is to bring the Love and Grace of Your Faith to your people, your community and our world. *Living Life as a Prayer* can affirm similarly. We can use such purpose statements as a touchstone for us to look to whenever we are making choices.

Asking often: "Do our actions (individually and collectively) emulate the action of bringing the Love and Grace of *Living Life as a Prayer* out into the world, into our neighborhoods, and in our families and close circles of friends?"

Be like the trees and have strength. We need to know that sometimes we will fail and sometimes the world is going to fail us. Each time we fail to live up to our purpose, may we strive to realign with it. Again, and again, and again. Knowing that as we do, as we mindfully focus on the mission of bringing Love and Grace out into the world, that we will be cultivating the strength of practices that serve our hearts and serve our Faith.

Be like the trees and have roots. Have we developed the roots in our faith and within our congregations and communities to be able to have inner strength and support systems when storms come, when tragedy strikes? Roots are the often unseen world beneath our thoughts, actions and deeds. Roots of faith, like roots of a forest, are labyrinths of communication networks that nurture us even as they inform and instruct our growth, and our ability to persevere. Even as they speak to the other inhabitants of this underground world.

Be like the trees and keep our lines of communication open. Just as the roots of trees speak to their neighboring trees, signaling them to provide for each other when they are in need. Ecologist Suzanne Simard tells us: *"A forest is a cooperative system," (Simard)* sharing resource transfers, signaling each other when specific nutrients are needed, and also signaling things like defense alerts and kin recognition and they form a symbiotic association with belowground fungi which are involved in the communication system as well.

A question for our congregations and communities to intentionally contemplate: Do we ensure Love and Grace are in symbiotic function to our lines of communication? It is wise to also consider what measures we have in place to make certain our communication signal is clear and that our transfer capacity for nutrients is optimal so that we can be safe and continue to grow.

Be like the trees and be flexible. Have we cultivated flexibility in our hearts and in our minds and in the ways we approach challenges? The kinds of challenges we face when we encounter differences in values, differences in opinions, differences in perspectives?

Be like the trees and let go. Just as the tree lets go of its leaves in Autumntime. When we encounter differences, are we open to letting go of the effort to be right? Are we able to let go of our resistance to change in order to make way for something different than we had imagined? Do we have the ability, perhaps more importantly do we have *the willingness,* to let go of something when its season has passed?

Be like the trees and breathe. For there are challenges that we can never make sense of. The frustrations of a system that cannot at present keep everyone safe. Are our hearts and minds able to remain open to breathe in Life and living even knowing that there are things *about* Life and living that we cannot begin to comprehend?

Be like the trees and allow our breath of Life. Allow our breath of Life to positively influence and even transform our wounded world. And transform each other.

And what of the comfort, and the artistry, of trees?

Be like the trees and provide shelter, and a place to call home. In what ways do we offer comfort and beauty and sanctuary? To each other and to our larger community? In what ways do we allow our radiance to be revealed? Our branches to be open in welcome to shelter all those who are seeking it?

Be like the trees and stretch. How far is our reach when we are seeking to serve in ways that demonstrate the Love and Grace of our Faith? To what lengths are we willing to go to to bring the Love and Grace of our Faith to the World?

What's OUR TREE? Individually? That's for each of us to determine. Collectively? We have claimed the Tree of Love, and of *Living Life as a Prayer.*

That's OUR TREE.

Individually we manifest *Living Life as a Prayer*, our individual trees, in the Orchard that is our congregation within varied chosen ministries and projects our members choose to participate:

- ☐ Hosting Vigils and Opportunities for Fellowship
- ☐ Clothing Drives, Food Cupboards and Community Gardens
- ☐ *The Grandmothers Circles*
- ☐ *Art Meditations*
- ☐ *Minerva Potlucks + Rituals*
- ☐ Hosting Retreats
- ☐ Leading small group ministries
- ☐ Evangelism
- ☐ Interfaith Community Connections
- ☐ Sunday services, and even coffee hour

Our actions in answering these calls with love demonstrate how we have claimed purpose of *Living Life as a Prayer* motivated by Love as our own, and, how this theology can claim us.

Living Life as a Prayer: That's Our Tree!

And that is how we how we move past the Afterward; that's how we move through it. And bring Love and Grace to the world in times of tragedy. And how we bring Love and Grace to each other; and even when we are standing in front of our mirrors.

Living Life as a Prayer

May we remember our covenants of love. May we create space to begin anew when what we have known has crumbled. When we grow weary of the brokenness, may we nurture and comfort each other. May we move in and out of our experienced worlds with Grace.

Let our words be gentle. Let our thoughts and our actions be consistent with the outcome we desire. Let our thoughts, our words and our deeds be rooted in manifestations of Love and Grace, and of *Living Life as a Prayer*. Let us remember who we are as a people and behave in a way that shows we do. Know that: When you lead with love, peace will follow.

May we love one another. And may we remember: Love will prevail. It will. It prevails every time we take the opportunity to wrap each other, and our world, in more love when tragedy strikes. It prevails every time our conversations and our actions in our communities and in our churches are about protecting the most vulnerable among us and building beloved community. Love prevails when we speak for love. When we stand for love. When we act for love. When we ARE Love. Love Prevails.

May we be like the trees and transform our world with every breath.

May we breathe in Love; and breathe out Strength.

May we breathe in Strength; and breathe out Grace.

May we breathe in Grace; and breathe out Love.

May we send light into the darkness. May we cradle the hearts of the heart-broken. May we discover together how to create a world where all are welcome and free and safe. May we *Live Life as a Prayer*.

Amen.

What if hospitality was the pillar of our Faith?

If coming together created sanctuary?

If sharing Joys and Sorrows was the path to enlightenment?

What if our sacred texts were our sermons, poems and songs?

If our principles were our doctrines?

If our covenant was the Hope that binds us?

Indeed, what if compassion presided over our thoughts and our deeds?

Living Life as a Prayer

OF AWE AND GRACE

"The Moment"
If there is a moment
When life
Is crystalized to destiny,
And the soul becomes
Suddenly immortal;
When a gesture beats
The first foot of an unending rhythm
And Being bursts into unquenchable flame - - -
Let this be it.

      (Sarton, 162/133)

Let us explore how to greet each day with gratitude and recognize miracles of all sizes, moment by moment.

Our human lives are made up of recognizable moments that render us in absolute awe of the miraculous we see before us.

Moments that catch us by surprise nestled in seemingly inauspicious conditions the touch of dew on the grass and flowers that greets us on our early morning springtime walks the glow of fireflies in soft summertime evenings clouds that descend like fog to roll over a mountain top in mid-autumn winter's first snow casting scenes as magical as a snow globe - the miniaturized landscape within the transparent sphere made manifest before our eyes in full scale and living color.

There are Moments mundane in their repetition, yet majestic nonetheless and eagerly greeted with awaited anticipation: Sunrise to *Sunset* to Moonrise to *Moonset*. Every single day these events occur. Yet when they do, their beauty has the ability to stop us in our tracks to just watch.

The cry of a newborn baby. The giggle of a young child. The first time a child rides their bike and a parent observes in awe. First kisses. Final goodbyes. Moment, by treasured moment, hailed by the Divine, by nature's call to attention, by Life's inevitable consequences of living uncanny and banal and we respond in *awe*.

My colleague *Rev. Cathie Stivers* is a scholar and translator. In her book, "Reviving Our Indigenous Souls, How to Practice the Ancient to Bring in the New," she artfully guides readers through the embodied ancient memory encoded in our souls that she says is hidden deep and dormant, yet active in our language in ways she takes time to delineate by going to the roots, origins, meanings and application of 31 common verbs that collectively capture the human experience.

> Proto-Indo-European, referred to as "PIE," is the linguistic reconstruction of the ancient common ancestor of the Indo-European languages, which the most widely spoken language family in the world, and of which English one.
>
> Etymology dates the oldest written roots back to the 4th millennium BC or earlier, associated with the prehistoric people of Eurasia.
>
> (Stivers)

Cathie is in alignment of belief among many mystics when she tells us that "In addition to the power of their ancestral lineage, our words also carry *energetic* power." (Stivers, 97) Two of those 31 words are Respond and Thank.

She says, "'*Respond*' comes from the Latin word '*respondere,*' meaning "answer to, promise in return: It is composed of *re-* ("back to the original place; again, anew, once more, against"), and '*-spond,*' from the Latin '*spondere*' ("to pledge"). This second half of the word comes from the Greek word '*spondeios,*' which is *"the name of the meter originally used in chants accompanying libations,"* and refers literally to a drink offering. It comes from the PIE root *"spend-, which means "to make an offering, perform a tire; engage oneself by a ritual act."* Cathie tells us, *"responding involves a relationship of deep reverence."* (Stivers, 94)

Further, "*Thank*' comes from the PIE root '**tong-*' ("to think, feel"), indicating that thanking is primarily an embodiment, and subsequently a verbal expression. To think and feel thanks is to be *grateful*. "Grateful" and "grace" both come from the PIE root '**gwere-*,' which means, "to favor." Cathie says, "*Our indigenous souls are keenly aware of the favor that was shown upon us by the Holies and the ancestors, who worked together diligently to bring us here.*"

She says, "*To be born in grace is to be intended, not random or accidental. It means there is a purpose for each of us; a place where we belong; and a people with whom we share our indebtedness. This is our original blessing, and so (the indigenous say) let all God's children say, 'Thank you.'*"

Thank you to that which we call Holy. *Thank you* to the miracles we recognize in the auspicious and the mundane. *Thank you* to each other.

Cathie assures us: "*Sooner* and *later*, both givers and receivers of thanks are transformed." And that: "*The more that gratitude is paid forward, the sooner it comes back to the original payer.*" Ultimately, gratitude enlightens us to the Universal Law of Oneness, as Hereditary Chief, Phil Lane Jr. explains:

"*When we strive to make our lives, every thought, word and action, a living Wopida [Dakota word for gratitude], we are given a great spiritual gift. For whenever our soul and the inmost chambers of our heart are filled with thanksgiving and gratitude it also naturally becomes filled with compassion, love, understanding, forgiveness, joy, happiness and oneness.*"

And in that space, *"There is no room for anything that separates ourselves and our oneness with our Beloved Creator, our Human Family and all Life, seen and unseen."* (Stivers, 144-145)

Meister Eckhart, the 13th Century theologian and mystic, said, *"If the only prayer you ever say in your entire life is 'thank you,' it will be enough."* (Stivers, 146)

My personal theology, and that which we teach at *The Church of Kineo*, is to *Live Life as a Prayer*. To cultivate a <u>practice</u> of reverence and gratitude. Life offers many moments for us to hone this practice. Two of my favorite rituals and most cherished communal memories stem from the honoring and reverence of the seasons milestones of change. On the East Coast, it is the Summer Solstice and first sunrise of the longest day. On the West Coast it is new year's eve and the last sunset of the year.

There is something about being in stillness with another person that is unlike being in action with them. Whether it is an intimate stillness shared by loves or a collective stillness shared in a group united in purpose. *Stillness quantified* <u>infuses power</u>.

This is the energy that sets the tone for the end of one year and the beginning of the next as friends of mine gather in La Jolla, California along with a few hundred other people at Nautilus by Windansea Surf Club for their annual celebration party. And a party is what it begins as late in the afternoon. There is a live band, tents, lots of activities, children running over the rocks, hardcore surfers catching a few last waves of the the year.

Then in the minutes before sunset, as if a cue had been given by an off-screen director, activities stop almost simultaneously. The children gathered to their parents, the musicians put down their instruments,

the vendors leave their tents, the surfers find their place in the watery line up and stay there.

And....

    Everyone

        Just

            Stops

And turns to face the Sun.

It is like that moment in the movie *City of Angels* when they recreate the legend of the angels who walk among us on Earth all gather together at sunrise and sunset. In the movie it was explained they gather because the fallen earth angels can still hear the music of their heavenly siblings and The Holy in the moments of sunrise and sunset. They are eager for that sensory experience. Longing for that long lost connection to the Divine. They gather. They turn toward the sun as it rises and as it falls. And they stand in stillness as the power of it greets them. *(Angels, 1998)*

At Windansea those present on New Year's Eve experience that feeling. Made even more palpable as the energy is received, responded to and shared by those present. Such an incredibly powerful way to release the old year and welcome the new one. So different than the exhilaration in the countdown to take place in Time Square when the ball drops. But, rather, filled with mindful, focused energy witnessing the Sun sink lower, and lower, and lower: descending to kiss the Earth. Those gather in gratitude for its presence.

And, in trust it will rise again.

Once the sun sets, the silence and the stillness last about a minute more. Awe engulfs the group. Reverence washes over and lingers tingling the skin. Grace presides for a moment as if frozen in time.

Then the anticipation meets reality bubbling over into jubilee as the entire group breaks into revelry: applause and cheers and yelling: *"Happy New Year!"* Hugging one another. Most smiling, even laughing. Some crying as the passing year, *as every year*, has brought with it both joys and sorrows, just as the new year, *as every year*, promises the same. It is magical. It feels like a miracle.

Yes, our human lives are made up of recognizable moments that render us in absolute awe of the miraculous we see before us. From interpersonal experiences and interactions, to miracles of all forms and sizes which appear in our lives, to this beautiful planet we live on. Tangible and incandescent. Life and living is a miracle.

May we remember in the words of Rev. Kate Braestrup, *"A miracle is not defined by an event. A miracle is defined by gratitude."* (Braestrup, 181)

The Theology of Rev. Twinkle Marie Manning

May we greet life's everyday miracles with reverence, giving thanks, *Living Life as a Prayer*, and be blessed with grace. Amen.

Living Life as a Prayer

Meditation

As we enter this time of prayer and meditation
I invite you to settle into your seats
Close your eyes if you wish
Allow your body to relax
Take a deep breath in and a long breath out
And again

Allow your mind to rest
and open to the awareness of just Being

Notice the miracles present in this moment
of quiet and stillness
Notice your breath
inhale to exhale
follow its repeating cycle
inhale to exhale

Notice your heart beat and pulse
Notice the sound of them,
the feel of them in your body
Notice the light that plays in the room
accessible to you even with your eyes closed
Notice your mind trying to
lead the way in this moment
in every moment

Inhale to exhale
And relax
And journey briefly to imagination

(Breathe)

Envision a beautiful wintery sunset
And the moon as it rises
Envision the pace of snowflakes
as they fill the sky
on a calm December evening
Follow one as it makes its way
slowly to the ground

Life
All around you
Life all within you

From the ground, to the snowflake, to the moon
as it passes the sun in the sky
This ritual of everyday miracles
Inhale to exhale
Welcome this moment of quiet and stillness.
(breathe)

Living Life as a Prayer

WEAVING HARMONY FROM WITHIN THE CHAOS

This chapter was originally prepared as a contemplative service in response to the Covid19 pandemic that shut down our churches in March of 2020. Musician Sarah Dan Jones wove in her "Breathing Meditation" with Rev. Manning's stream of conscience words of reflection. The service opened and closed with the two parts of Angela Morgan's poem, "Kinship."

KINSHIP by Angela Morgan (part 1)

I am aware,

As I go commonly sweeping the stair,

Doing my part of the every-day care —

Human and simple my lot and my share —

I am aware of a marvelous thing:

Voices that murmur and ethers that ring

In the far stellar spaces where cherubs sing.

I am aware of the passion that pours

Down the channels of fire through Infinity's doors;

Forces terrific, with melody shod.

Music that mates with the pulses of God.

The Theology of Rev. Twinkle Marie Manning

I am aware of the glory that runs
From the core of myself to the core of the suns.
Bound to the stars by invisible chains.
Blaze of eternity now in my veins.
Seeing the rush of ethereal rains
Here in the midst of the every-day air —
I am aware.

Sufi Mystic, Hazrat Inayat Khan, taught that Harmony is the medium between God and humans. That there is a kind of peace for which each soul seeks that corresponds to the resonance of the Divine. Yet while the goal sought is that of reaching peace, that once achieved this peace results in Harmony. Such Harmony is the embodiment of Heaven on Earth. And the lack of such Harmony is that which humans experience as Hell. To attain Harmony is to be in union with that which we identify as Holy. And we experience such Harmony as peace. Peace in our hearts. Peace in our Minds. Peace that we witness made manifest in our lives in all kinds of ways.

"When I breathe in, I'll breathe in peace."

Intrinsic wisdom has written such awareness indelibly into our natures. Coded with this spiritual DNA we are equipped to intuitively assess situations.

"When I breathe out, I'll breathe out love."

When what we recognize as disharmony materializes, especially when the disharmony creates physical isolation from the people we love, the places we like to spend time, and the routines and rituals we've organized our lives around, we can feel deeply disconnected. Disconnected from that which we hold dear. Disconnected from our own self assuredness and self awareness. Disconnected from where we draw our faith.

"Breathe in, Breathe out."

This disconnected feeling feels like chaos to us. Disrupting the harmony we recognize as holy. As sacred. As safe.

"Breathe in, Breathe out."

Yet if we can still the emotional storm that is rising. If we can locate calmness in our bodies, in our beings, we can restore the harmony.

"When I breathe in, I'll breathe in peace."

If we open to the eternal wisdom we have access to, and we actively allow ourselves to accept uncertainty into this moment. We can reset. We can focus on the things within our control.

"When I breathe out, I'll breathe out love."

Moment by moment, thought by thought, breath by breath.

"Breathe in, Breathe out."

We can recognize the ways in which goodness still exists. We turn our attention to the sacred and mundane before us - wherever we are. And feel the blessings of both.

"Breathe in, Breathe out."

And as we cultivate this practice of weaving harmony from within the chaos, we become the conductor in the symphony of our emotions. This does not mean the chaos disappears entirely. Nor that we receive answers we like to all the things we have questions about. But it makes space, intentionally so, for us to navigate effectively within what Life has presented us with. And within such space, unimaginable beauty is often found to exist.

"When I breathe in, I'll breathe in peace.

When I breathe out, I'll breathe out love.

When I breathe in, I'll breathe in peace.

When I breathe out, I'll breathe out love.

When I breathe in, I'll breathe in peace.

When I breathe out, I'll breathe out love.

Breathe in, Breathe out.

Breathe in, Breathe out.

Breathe in, Breathe out." (Jones)

KINSHIP by Angela Morgan (part 2)

I am aware,
As I sit quietly here in my chair.
Sewing or reading or braiding my hair —
Human and simple my lot and my share —
I am aware of the systems that swing
Through the aisles of creation on heavenly wing,
I am aware of a marvelous thing:
Trail of the comets in furious flight,
Thunders of beauty that shatter the night,
Terrible triumph of pageants that march
To the trumpets of time through Eternity's arch.
I am aware of the splendor that ties
All the things of the earth with the things of the skies,
Here in my body the heavenly heat.
Here in my flesh the melodious beat
Of the planets that circle Divinity's feet.
As I sit silently here in my chair,
I am aware.

May we carry with us the light of awareness that we are not alone; we are connected to one another by a love so strong and so bright that its flame is eternal. May we *Live Life Like a Prayer*. Amen.

BLESSING

May you be ever vigilant in your self-care.

May you take moments each day to reflect on the most positive aspects of your lives.

May you find ways to reach out to those who are most vulnerable

And if you are of the most vulnerable

May you ask for and accept help as it arrives

And may you have peace in your minds, harmony in your hearts.

And my beloveds,

May you be blessed as you most assuredly are a blessing to the world.

Amen and Blessed Be.

Living Life as a Prayer

AWAKENING WISDOM TO SABBATICAL LIVING

> This sermon was originally written in response to the Covid19 pandemic situation, yet also as a response to the idea that anything before the pandemic was "normal." As a society, we've lost our way. We've created systems that are counter intuitive to the well-being of our members. The idea and ideals of a Sabbatical Lifestyle are worth consideration as it aligns with the practices of Living Life as a Prayer.

What if there was nothing wrong with this moment? What if this congregation-wide, community-wide, state-wide, nation-wide, world-wide physical isolation was our choice.

True, in the part of the world where we reside, it is our choice to certain degrees whether or not we abide the CDC recommendations of physical isolation. Most *are* abiding and choosing to keep themselves and others safe with their choice of Sheltering in Place. Even so, most if not all of us, wish we did not have to choose to do so.

Many wish life could just go on as usual. That we could come and go as we please, to the places of business and places of worship we are accustomed to. That we could visit or travel to where and with whom we wish, at a moment's notice or as previously scheduled. And many if not most, have expressed that there is no way this will be the permanent "new normal."

But, what if even without there being a pandemic, without there being a reason to be fearful of being in close physical proximity to our friends, our congregation members, our neighbors and co-workers...

What if we chose this period of time all on our own with the express intention of not just physical isolation, but of Intentional Being. Being in solitude. Being in the company of only those we wish to share a home with.

What if every year we determined that we would *rest* in place. What if every year we chose to take a *sabbatical* from the constructs of the material and materialistic world and how it functions.

What if we selected a period of time each year where we opted to not go shopping, or meet for lattes, or attend in-person public gatherings and events? What if we could work part of the year <u>instead of all of it</u> and still have financial security? What if much if not most or even all of the time we could work from home with out having to extend resources on commuting?

What if our lives included a season where we turn inward. A contemplative time. A season where we focus on the nurturing our souls and of our closest relationships. Yes! What if we decided to spend our time exclusive, dedicated, intentional *extended* time Sheltered in Place. Being in the company of only those dearest to us. What if we had time to prepare for that.

What if as we went about the work of everyday life throughout most of the year, we were also planning and looking forward to such a sabbatical time.

Prior to the pandemic shutdowns such mode of living, such a lifestyle, would have perhaps been more difficult to imagine. Maybe even impossible to imagine. Yet, now, with so many of us separated from family we love, and with much stress about resources being depleted, how much easier addressing the concerns of the virus would have been, had we been already of the mindset of incorporating a sabbatical lifestyle.

That's not say the whole world would shut down at once. But rather, if enough of us were to determine this kind of *Season of Sabbatical* was important to include in our *Wheel of the Year,* even necessary to include for our own wellbeing, we could *and would* collaboratively calendar in such time through out the year in such a way where "Essential Services" were maintained, and where "Essential Personnel" seamlessly rotated into and out of their work time and sabbatical time.

We would not be the first human tribe to establish *a time of rest* into our schedule. To varying degrees our ancestors and cultures each assigned periods of rest. And, to some extent still do.

For millennia Christian and Jewish traditions, for example, kept and still keep the Sabbath, a day of rest - every 7th day. The concept of an extended sabbatical dates back to Ancient agricultural peoples who minded instructions to rest from working their fields every seven years - for a whole year *they rested.* To nurture the fields, and to nurture their bodies, minds, and spirits. They rested their fields; they rested themselves.

Nowadays sabbaticals have become institutionalized for the tenured and the elite. Our professors, our clergy. Yet not, for the most part, the rest of the work force who get at best two weeks vacation each year - *if they take it*. By the time they are beginning to unwind, just when their bodies are adjusting to a more relaxed setting, they are due to return to their hectic work schedules.

Some sophisticated modern-day companies have researched and affirmed the importance of extended time off from work to ensure employees creativity and health. Medical studies - *and common sense* - align with this. Telling us that extended periods of rest from work and from stress and from..."doing" result in lower blood pressure and longevity of life.

How much happier and healthier we would be if we *simplified* our lives in this way!

In her book, *"Reviving Our Indigenous Souls, How to Practice the Ancient to Bring in the New,"* Rev. Cathie Stivers explains the word *"simplify"* - from its original root words and context - literally means *"to put things together as one, in a braided, folded way."* That to simplify is to weave together similar things into a fabric of one.

If in the fabric of our human lives we built our organizations, our communities, our nations, with the sentiment that we are indeed One, we would begin to weave together lifestyles, and cultures, and ways of being that support, and lift up, nurture and nourish such Oneness. For everyone.

We would install extended times of rest and enrichment. We would be_ready to Shelter in Place without anxiousness or restlessness. We would practice physical isolation from the world around us as a Holy time, a Sacred time. A Blessing.

Hmmm...For now, we are where we are. Some of us are blessed to be

in climate controlled comfortable homes, sharing our space with those we love and who love us. We have plenty of food, fresh water, needed supplies, and we have access to replenish these as needed. We have connection to the outside world via internet audio and video technologies. We have cell phones and televisions and radios to keep us informed and entertained. We have books and art in our homes. *We have music.*

Here in Maine, with the vastness and beauty of Nature all around us, we have the privilege of being able to access the outdoors. We can travel down country lanes, be still in our yards and parks, hike in the woods. All seasons of the year! Some are able snowshoe and cross country ski. And as Winter's long season catches up to Spring, we have access to kayak and boat in our lakes and rivers throughout the warmer seasons.

Mindfully so, respecting the parameters around the spaces of others desiring to do the same.

We are indeed fortunate here. Yes, some, hopefully many, of us are safe, and happy, active, socially if not physically connected, and even grateful, some of us deeply so, for this extended time of closeness together with those we love. For this extended time of spaciousness within our own lives.

Others are not in such comfortable, loving, or safe environments. Many in our region, and throughout our country and certainly around the world are struggling financially, physically and emotionally.

Hourly workers are being laid off, others are being furloughed, or impacted by alternate work schedule structures businesses are implementing to be able to stay afloat. To be able to offer jobs at all. Individuals and families are stressed with little ones at home with them, full time now. There is little to no access to the mental wellness practitioners and tools to help guide them through these challenges.

Parents with young children and those care-giving in their homes for the elderly, parents, grandparents and others. Also those who may have special needs or who are caring for those with special needs. They are not getting sufficient rest nor relief from duties. Alternately, many of us are separated from our dearest loved ones by virtue of geography. *For example, two of our adult children, a son-in-law, and three grandchildren reside in Canada. With the borders closed, we cannot physically be together. It is heart-wrenching and a hardship to be separated from our family.*

Indeed, amplified by the pandemic, these are trying times. People are homeless. Children are confined in abusive homes. Still others, are seeking to access the things that make *their* daily life more tolerable, manageable, that may be *essential to them* but those items may not be on the state-mandated "essential" list, so access is difficult to access if not impossible for the foreseeable future. Increasing the stress. Increasing the loneliness.

Yes, loneliness. Even, and perhaps especially, for those *"Sheltered" in Place*, in a space that doesn't feel like *Shelter* at all. That is not a Haven, but their own personal hell. There is the face of loneliness. There the most vulnerable among us reside.

For those of us who use the language of prayer, we pray that those who have fallen ill to the virus, recover swiftly. We pray many will never have this virus at all. We pray that those living in unsafe places are kept safe. We pray that those have lost loved ones are able to have measures of peace in their hearts and minds as they cope with their grief. We pray that cures are found for that which cause suffering. For those who do not use the language of prayer, indeed wish this were simply so.

We are in this together. The illnesses that plague humankind, the challenges Earth's residence face. These impact us all. Especially in moments of uncertainty. Especially during a pandemic when we do not know the extent of the outcome, nor how long this isolation it will last.

How do we get through it? As one of my favorite author's to quote, Anne Lamott says, *"Bird by Bird."*

I smile as I recall this in her book of the same name, *Bird by Bird*, Anne tells us the childhood story of her brother who decades ago, ten years old at the time, was trying to complete a written school report on birds. It was due the next day. He had had three months to prepare and write it.

She recalls they were at their family cabin, and her brother close to tears, sitting at their kitchen table. He had his binder, paper and pencils and piles of unopened books about birds all around him. He was immobilized. Such a daunting task ahead of him. Three months of work to do *in a single day*. He wondered how on earth he was going to get through it?

Their father sat down beside him. He place his arm around his son's shoulder, and gently said, *"Bird by bird, buddy. Just take it bird by bird." (Lamott)*

And that is how we are all going to get through this moment. This daunting moment of uncertainty.

Bird by bird;

Step by step;

Task by task;

Day by day;

Moment by moment.

Amen. And may it be so.

Living Life as a Prayer

LOVE THE LAND YOU'RE WITH

Deep in the forest,

Quiet shapes the sound of immense emollient twilight.

Saturated shades of perpetual green caress the sky;

Blues sink down to violet.

Leaves land lightly;

   Layering lanes to linger upon.

Seekers of silence satisfied,

Within this modulating animated tenement.

Sanctuary of Solace found beneath copious canopies of trees;

Living, Breathing.

"Love the land you're with" embodies the relationship I have with Nature. For many years I lived beside or within walking distance to the ocean. I resonate to this day with Her rhythms, finding both strength and healing there.

This remained true of the Atlantic and the Pacific, from Florida to Canada, California to Hawaii. Each place I have lived, I immersed in her wisdom. The

Oceans' sandy beaches and weathered cliffs provide long moments of reflection and inspiration. The metaphysical aspects of my soul opened in Her presence.

Later in my life I moved inward. As I type I realize this is both a literal and symbolic way of describing my ever-evolving transformation and awakening. Inland I found lakes and mountains that have grounded me in this place in Time, while providing me insights on the legacies of those who came before me, and the ones that will follow. In their stillness and aliveness, the mountains, the lake, our land and trees that surround us guide me to embrace a deeper connection with Earth and with Spirit. Inland Life has provided me with the opportunity to grow and to harvest, again both physically and symbolically, as I work with the soil of the Land. I am nurtured and more nurturing here.

Here are some glimpses of our sacred places on Moosehead Lake in Maine:

Living Life as a Prayer

> The global pandemic has highlighted something fascinating. It is estimated that:
> - Hawaii has a seven day food supply.
> - New York has a four day food supply.
> - Los Angeles has a three day food supply.
>
> *Zack Bush, MD, August 19th, 2020*

I am putting the finishing touches on this manuscript during the 2020 pandemic. Many are noticing what many others have been prophesying, and that is, that we need to get back to our roots, get closer to nature, learn to cultivate the land, even as we need to cultivate our spirituality. Dr. Zach Bush, with expertise in Internal Medicine, Endocrinology and Metabolism, and Hospice/Palliative care, candidly states that,

"The global pandemic has highlighted something fascinating. It is estimated that: Hawaii has a seven day food supply. New York has a four day food supply. Los Angeles has a three day food supply.

If you think about it, we are becoming aware of how we are all living on figurative islands. More than 95% of the food coming into LA or NYC is brought in by long distance trucking freight. An estimated 30% of the traffic on the George Washington Bridge in NYC is food delivery trucks.

We are not just island cities, we are island homes... Take a moment to consider that 50% of Americans were farming in 1880. Now less than 2% of the nation is employed in agriculture. From another perspective, in 1945 Americans grew 40% of their food in their backyard gardens. Now we grow 0.1% of our food in our backyards.

The logistics of Island reality actually now apply everywhere because we've outsourced everything; we have supply chains for toilet paper and surgical masks that wrap 12,000 miles around the world." (Bush)

This evidence of this vast supply chain cycle is seen clearly here in Maine where we have abundant resources that leave us wanting for very little. Yet we do not have access to these resources in ways that are most beneficial to those who live here. Maine's woodlands, for example, are used to produce building materials, furnishings, paper products, ornaments and more. Instead of primarily producing locally, we export much of the wood for manufacturing to then turn around and import the needed products, often at a reduced quality and with quantities depending not on local need, but on the will of the foreign manufacturer. It is deeply unfortunate and a detriment to our communities as a whole.

Likewise with our power sources of wind, hydro and solar. These should serve our local communities first, rather than be gathered in their places of origin, bypass the local communities, and be shipped off to be utilized by other regions and states. Most every state, province and region in North America, and I suspect, the world, have similar stories to tell. It is counter-intuitive to operate this way. It is a flaw in the system that has come into the spotlight during this pandemic as people throughout are scrambling to access these very resources from which the root source originates in their communities, yet the end product is produced on the other side of the world. Creating a more balanced and cause effective system where we produce and manufacture the items our communities need locally is one of the solutions many are beginning to see as prudent.

It is also a natural side effect of living a lifestyle that is close to nature. Such a lifestyle will lend itself to the cultivation of practices, spiritual and otherwise, that are in alignment with our environments.

The pandemic is a call to turn inward, not just spiritually, but physically, inward toward our homes, and with our communities. It is a call to stop outsourcing the necessities of life and to renew homesteading ideals as families and as neighbors. This need not be a fearful idea, for it is something that can and should be achieved at the community level. Households sharing with one another that which they grow in their gardens, harvest from their fields, and gather from the lands they reside.

Wherever you call home, connect completely in the beauty of Nature. Find ways to touch and tend to the land. If you can grow food in the soil, do so. And, if possible, allow that food to be your primary source of nourishment, or at least a part of each of your meals. The skills of foraging are useful as well, and many essential items can be derived from such native industries. Creating networks within your families and communities and neighboring communities to share the abundance of what you grow, gather and manufacture, foster an expansive and consciously interconnected environment locally.

For your own edification and balancing, develop rituals and routines that connect you directly with the natural elements around you. If you live near a water source, immerse yourself in it if possible, swim in it, boat and kayak and sail on it, or at least touch it regularly. Sit at the shore of the water weekly or daily if possible. It has tales to tell for those willing to listen. As does the wind, and the moon as it rises and sun as it sets. Your unique place on this planet offers you great insights into the rhythms of Nature and the mysteries of the Universe.

Get to know the creatures you inhabit this place with. Recognize the rhythms of their activities in each season. Notice how *your* rhythms vary from season to season. Feel the energies that are unique to this landscape. The plants, the trees, the way the water moves. Notice how you feel, how your energy resonates here.

Love the land you are with, and it will love you.

Emergent Green

Green like no other;
spectrums full,
lengths of trees adorned in
pigments persuaded by daylight,
tilt toward yellow.

Spring has arrived;
Summer soon to follow;
Life in Maine as it should be.

What questions must we ask
to realize our purpose?
Can we know the unknown?
Can we seek the unsearchable?

Green like no other;
spectrums full,
lengths of trees adorned in
pigments persuaded by daylight,
tilt toward yellow.

Could that we would
understand what's before us;
unspeakable majesty awaits
the awakening soul.

Living Life as a Prayer

OFFERINGS AND STEWARDSHIP

For as long as we live in a monetized society, the places we worship, and the people for whom leading the worship is their work, it is important that their communities support and lift up such work monetarily.

Tithing is an ancient practice that has merit. Some religions issue a mandatory 10% minimum tithe, while others implement strategic levels of participation and elitism within their ranks, with members paying accordingly.

At *The Church of Kineo*, in response to *Living Life as a Prayer*, we ask that you donate from your heart what you can towards this work. We ask that your tithing not be a hardship for you, but also not be a pittance. May your tithing be as much as you can reasonably offer in support of the work in your community, and in the efforts of sharing the spiritual practice of *Living Life as a Prayer* so it serves many others near and far.

Gifts of spirit strengthen our hearts and minds.

Gifts of service broaden the outreach and ministries of this congregation.

Gifts of time create measurable milestones and time honored traditions.

Gifts of money sustain this building, programs offered here and make it possible for us to live into our mission.

We gratefully accept your gifts.

Living Life as a Prayer

OPEN HANDS - LIVING LIFE AS A PRAYER

"Imagine all the people
Living for today...
Imagine all the people
Living life in peace...
Imagine all the people
Sharing all the world..."

(Lennon, 1971)

Written by John Lennon the year I was born, *"Imagine"* was one of the first songs my father would sing to me; one of the last songs to play before we laid my brother to rest 23 years ago. One of the most popular songs in our peace and social justice movements. Imagine. One of the hopes that I believe we each carry with us. One of the hopes that I believe draws us to worship together each week. One of the hopes that beckons us towards lives of social activism and standing on the side of love.

But how do we, practical and truly, transform this imagined dream into reality? I believe it is by *Living Life as a Prayer*. With open hands and minds rooted in the inherent worth and dignity of every person. This is an integral piece, indeed the essential piece, of Möbius Living.

Imagine you have a gift beside you that you wish to give to a beloved friend. Now clench your fists. Is it easy to hold and handle the gift you wish to give so as to pass it to your friend? Imagine your friend's fists are also clenched. Is it easy for your friend to receive the gift into his or her own hands? Perhaps your friend has a gift for you as well. Imagine how clumsily the interaction, the gift exchange, would be. If the gift were precious, perhaps even fragile, with clenched fists you run the added risk dropping the gift, and breaking it. Now, open your hands. Feel the difference?

Know this: Every interaction we have is an opportunity to give a gift. How much easier to give and to receive when our hands are open to giving and receiving. And it is not just our hands. Feel what happens in your body when you clench your hands. What happens in your arms, your chest, your back, your spine, your face? Do you also notice a clenching of your mind, of your heart?

Now open your hands. Feel the difference? Feel the difference in your body. So often when we encounter - difficult people - and when we face challenges and disappointments, and especially setbacks in our lives, we do so with *clenched fists*.

Clenched everything!

Something happens, or *someone* does *or says* something that is upsetting to us, *and we clench*. A bracing for impact, in an unregulated tendency of shoring up our senses. Only, instead of strengthening our senses, our automatic clenching reinforces barriers. Barriers that inhibit our ability to see with clarity. Barriers that prevent pathways to transformation and to peace.

This clenching also activates resistance. Resistance to curiosity. Resistance to being flexible. Resistance to learning more about a situation or person. Resistance to better understanding each other, and even ourselves.

Possibilities evaporate when our hearts and minds are closed. No gifts can be shared, *given or received*, with fists (or minds or hearts or spirits *or even ideals*) clenched.

A word about gifts: It has been said that you cannot give a gift you do not posses. Worse, when you try, if the gift you are attempting to give is not yours to give, not within you to give, it is a false gift and potentially dangerous. To both the giver and the receiver of the gift. For instance, if the gift is given in a form that *resembles* Love or charity, yet in reality is founded in enmity or arrogance, neither love nor abundance can grow from such a gift. And the result will be a depletion of energy, and of trust, in both the giver and the receiver of the gift.

If we want our gift to be given and received like a prayer, then we need to inhabit the reality of *Living Life as a Prayer*. To do that, first, we need to decide what kind of prayer we want to be.

The sources we draw our faith from offer many insights to what we could include in our own unique description of what *Living Life as a Prayer* could be to us as congregations, as communities of people, and as individuals.

In chapters six and seven of the Bible book of *Matthew* we are given a model for *Living Life as a Prayer* It is here the Golden Rule of doing unto others as you would have them do unto you was birthed as Jesus urges us:

"So in everything, do to others what you would have them do to you, for this sums up the Law and the Prophets." (Matthew 7:12)

We are cautioned in these chapters of the Bible against judging others. We are encouraged to ask for guidance when we need it. He suggests for us to give generously to those less fortunate than us and to do this giving without pious arrogance. He also tells us it is important to not be greedy; to not hoard the blessings and gifts we have. He says to not be hypocritical - saying or doing something outwardly that we do not feel in our hearts. He points out that gratitude is integral to prayer.

Being deeply grateful for our blessings and expressing this thanks. And, forgiveness. Matthew says to ask for forgiveness when we have failed to do our best. And to grant forgiveness when others have failed to do their best. Also, he tells us to not worry excessively about living, about having our needs met. Another important aspect to our own unique expression of *Living Life as a Prayer* could include being mindful stewards of our Earth, and the other beings residing here with us.

The foundation for *Living Life as a Prayer*, is having a relationship with the Divine. It is a treasure beyond compare to any other. This Holy relationship is one that is rooted in quiet contemplation and connection and is revealed by each of us in the ways we live our lives in the world. One such indicator of how we are living in the world is noted a few chapters later, in Matthew 12:31 where he proclaims that the second greatest commandment of all is to love our neighbor as our self.

Cultivating a sacred and personal connection to that which we call Holy, and abiding purposefully, faithfully the principle of loving our neighbor as our self. These are cornerstones to *Living Life as a Prayer*.

When we live life as a prayer, our reactions to situations and to people become subtle, even unconscious, manifestations of the prayer we bring in to the world. This can be a process of strategically aligning our thoughts and feelings, actions and responses through contemplative practices toward how we want to experience the Divine, experience the Holy, experience God, even how we want to experience the World. And, how we want *others* to experience *us*.

It can also be a letting go. An Opening of the hands, of the mind, of the heart, *of the spirit* so as to welcome in the embodiment of the Divine into our hands, our minds, our hearts, and our spirits.

By doing this we enter and merge with what can be called The Holy Quiet. The place of Being that is within us, and through us, and beyond us. By practice and by surrender, prayer becomes co-created with the Divine, and with others. And *The Holy Quiet* becomes part of our daily lives.

As a result, as we embody *Living Life as a Prayer*, we shed feelings of inadequacies, feelings of not being good enough. Also, we shed feelings of having to prove our rightness and righteousness to others, and to ourselves. In doing so we are liberated from self-imposed doctrines and societal impositions of dogmatic correctness.

Doctrines? Dogma? Oh Yes! While we may have a faith tradition that prides itself on being free of antiquated dogma, and while our doctrines, we believe, are inspired, inherent and beneficial to *Living Life as a Prayer*, each one of us come filled to the brim with our own doctrines and dogma. Ones we inherited for good or for ill from our families. Ones we adopted often as protective layers in reaction to sorrows we experienced; and ones as tenets from the social environments we choose to be a part of.

Much of these internalized dogmas and doctrines we keep hidden from the world, and from each other, for we do not want to be judged for them. And, they can be even hidden from ourselves,for they are sources of pain, or at least points of opposition juxtaposed to who we actually want to be in the world. And who we want to be for each other.

Yet, when we live life as a prayer, we renounce inherited and internalized doctrines, dogmas and tenets and begin to emulate our personal credos though our words and our actions. More than that, deeper than that, we begin to recognize the beauty blossoming in our own hearts and minds. And as that beauty blossoms, we recognize with clarity the callings of our heart; the Callings from God.

And it is this, hearing and answering our callings, which transforms our otherwise transient lives into union with the Divine. This union becomes evident in the transfiguration of our thoughts, and our emotions.

And when this happens we no longer need to clench when faced with challenging situations *or people*. Because we know the inherent truth of our own hearts and minds. We feel our union with the that which we call Holy. And, we are eager to reveal this beautiful truth, this beautiful prayer-full life, with others.

Living Life as a Prayer, we are open and accessible, so others can look into our hearts and see that which we revere. They see what New Thought and liberal religious forefather James Martineau describes as *"soliloquies of the unguarded mind." (Martineau,* 56)

When this is visible, our authenticity is no longer hidden. And, our gifts, when shared with open hands, are recognized for all the love they contain.

When we live life as a prayer, we not only believe in our founding principle of the inherent worth and dignity of every person. We practice it. We become open to seeing the soliloquies of the hearts and minds of those we encounter who are most challenging to us. We extend to such ones the same compassion and curiosity we would hope they would extend to us for the anomalies we *surely must be* to them.

When we live life as a prayer, our actions uphold and support the belief in, and realization of, *the inherent worth and dignity of every person* even if, and especially *when*, every person does not do the same for us.

When we live life as a prayer, we model with sincerity the sentiment of Universalist poet, Edwin Markham when he says:

"He drew a circle that shut me out--

Heretic, a rebel, a thing to flout.

But Love and I had the wit to win:

We drew a circle

that took him in!" (Markham)

Yes, we draw a circle that takes them in. For this is how we love our neighbors as our selves. This is how we live life as a prayer. If we choose to meet obstacles and differences of opinions, *even ones that seem fundamentally opposed* and present challenges beyond the obvious. If we choose to meet them not with clenched fists but, rather, with open hands, open minds and open hearts. This is how we live into the principle of *the inherent worth and dignity of every person.* Every person. This is how we bring into reality *the dream* we Imagine.

"You may say I am a dreamer;

But I am not the only one.

I hope someday you'll join us;

And the world will be as one." (Lennon, 1971)

If we are to realize this dream, the one we all long for; the one we each strive for as we pick up the mantles of social justice and of inclusion and of freedom. The dream we imagine of a world in peace; a community united; a community of love; it starts here.

Here. In our hearts and in our congregations and in our faith communities, and with our neighbors, especially the ones we disagree with. If we find the circle that our neighbors draw is one that shuts us out, Then

Living Life as a Prayer

the circle we are called to draw Is a circle that draws them in. That invites and welcomes and is curious. The circle of love. In recognition of the inherent worth and dignity of every person.

For the road to peace is the way of peace. And the path to prayer is the path of prayer. This is the fire of commitment we need to covenant with each other and with God. This is the merging that must take place of our hearts with our callings.

The Theology of Rev. Twinkle Marie Manning

Summary

Living Life as a Prayer (and Möbius Living as the way of building The Beloved Community) is uniquely tied to the understandings we have about our Universal existence and the practices we inculcate into our lives. This book led an exploration into this theory and demonstrates with clarity and enthusiasm that The Beloved Community will heal the pervading feelings of separateness and loneliness that exists in our world. Indeed, we can see clearly how *Living Life as a Prayer*, contemplatively and practically, can permeate the structures of our reality to create The Beloved Community we seek to be made manifest.

Living Life as a Prayer reengages us with the ultimate Truths that the Universe's function receives our cooperation in its co-creation, and that we are all Universally connected to Source, and to each other. When we understand these Truths, we are in a position to observe and interact consciously. We see how coincidences purposefully coincide. We become mindful with our thoughts, feelings and behaviors. We begin to realize that we each carry a Divine Echo that connects us to the primal Source and that these Echoes we carry are in constant recognition of each other. We begin to understand that each person is not only a mirror of our Soul, but indeed, our Anam Ċara, our Soul Friend. From this understanding, we interact with others in acknowledgement of the inherent worth and dignity of every person. As we do this, we begin to experience positive shifts in our relationships that reflect this knowing.

With wonder and appreciation we live out our days always, and all ways, being present to the awareness that we are blessed to be living on holy ground, in sacred time and place, with every encounter with one another being those of divine nature. This deep gratitude and reverence for life motivates us in dedicating focus and attention towards cultivating the essential practices of a mindful Möbius Lifestyle and *Living Life as a Prayer*. We direct the 2.5 watts available in every heart beat towards the co-creation of The Beloved Community from the inside out and the outside in.

We also become acutely aware of that which would detract us from our highest good: the external and internal negative influences that if left unchecked could perpetuate suffering in our lives, and in the lives of those we love. We know that we are complicit to the suffering of others if we do not attain the ability to listen and understand those we love. We are also complicit when we make choices that are not in alignment with True Love and attentive to *Living Life as a Prayer*.

Conscientious of these principles, we begin to shape our relationships with thoughtfulness and curiosity. We seek to discover what ways those we love wish to receive Love, and, with intention, we learn to provide Love in the ways most desired by those we love. We also learn to ask for Love in the ways we most wish to receive it. These vulnerable interactions build trust, build respect, and build The Beloved Community.

As we attune to the energies of influence, we make modifications to bring us closer to our desired outcomes. Things once hidden to us are no longer concealed. As such, we perceive our own negatively entrenched patterns, some inherited, some chosen, that do not serve our best interest. We dissolve and transform these into more positive habits as we strengthen our practices with meditations, rituals and actions that deliberately support our *Living Life as a Prayer*.

We summon the willpower and faith to develop practices in alignment with how we most wish to live our daily lives. Most importantly, we turn to that which we call Holy and surrender to it knowing that we are not alone. We affirm that our purpose is to Love and to be loved, and we make this a priority above all else in our lives. Our connections with each other and to Source are the foundations from which we build The Beloved Community.

From this place of awareness, knowing we are loved and loving and connected, we lend ourselves to the forward motion of the Universe. We become fully open to exploring authentic human experiences, including that of our sacred sexuality in full understanding of the importance of deep intimacy and frequent physical and spiritual sexual activity as intrinsic to our nature, and of utmost significance to our Being and our well-being. All this emboldens us to step into our roles as leaders and stewards of transformation and healing. Uninhibited by limitations that negate our divinity, the energetic fullness we bring forward into our community as a result of our spiritual sophistication in reclaiming and embodying our sacred sexuality creates positive ripple affects that will strengthen The Beloved Community. Ultimately we discern that there exists a place in our hearts where intimacy has no limit and love has no barrier. And it is from within this place that we *Live Life as a Prayer*.

Deepening our understanding about Möbius Living, we immerse ourselves in the belief that our lives are Art. We awaken to the knowledge that seeming mistakes can transform into something even more beautiful than we could have ever imagined. We are gentle with ourselves and with each other, offering forgiveness as we journey together. Möbius Living and *Living Life as a Prayer* understands the centrifugal forces at work, and feels the pull towards center, the root and connectivity of all things. As we become attuned to the ebbs and flows of the energies present within and around us, we are galvanized to engage in Life, and in living, fully.

Understanding Time, too, is Möbius, yet not becoming distracted by its amorphous nature. Rather, we embrace our physical and spiritual experiences of Time. Making every moment count even as we know every choice matters, we choose carefully. We honor our deepest desires for connection with the Holy, and with each other. Intelligently and intuitively, we arrange our time with the people in our lives, and with our connection to that which we call Holy, in ways that demonstrate we value them.

Living Life as a Prayer

There are many paths, practices and principles we can explore and master within The Beloved Community. We can choose, as Rev. Dave Ruffin suggests, to embody a Pentecostal Practice of Transcendence. Meaning, cultivating a co-creative practice that opens us up for a direct encounter with the transcendent, experiencing the mystery with the Holy, every day of our lives.

We can heed the experiential wisdom of Rev. Marlin Lavanhar by living in this world with the knowledge that we need to be asking the right questions and be prepared with answers and actions that emulate our callings. In times of sorrow, we can remember that *because* bad things happen, we are called to be instruments of Love. And, *when* bad things do happen, we can choose to be those instruments of Love. And, when good things happen, we can refine our practices of being instruments of Love. Love is never passive in *Living Life as a Prayer*. It is always active.

As we proactively envision healing the loneliness that exists in the world, we engage in spiritual evangelism, as taught by Rev. Ian White Maher, with the loving motive of offering life changing joy to others. As we do this, we model unconditional welcome and radical hospitality, with open hearts, minds and spirits. And, when we do that, we begin to see ever more clearly that when we bless someone, everything in our life changes. In this way we, too, reveal our authenticity and grant others access to the soliloquies of our unguarded minds. Indeed, we are open and accessible, so others can look into our hearts and see that which we revere.

Discerning these principles, we understand the complicated simplicity of Love: that Love at its core is alive and curious. Love wants only to love. When the gift we give is Love, unconditionally, the gift we receive is the ability to hear our own callings, resoundingly. When we hear our callings, we hear the messages the Universe has been sending all along and we can respond accordingly. This is the Life *Lived as a Prayer*.

In its holistic shaping of The Beloved Community, *Living Life as a Prayer* teaches us to be vigilant about what we are nurturing from the inside out, and the outside in. We seek, and find, and share *The Holy Quiet* as it becomes part of our lived experience. *Living Life as a Prayer* is indeed the Way of Building The Beloved Community for it embraces the wholeness of us; the wholeness of each other, to heal, to experience, to guide, and to Love.

The essential teaching of *Living Life as a Prayer* is that we model our lives to co-create the world we imagine: a peaceful planet; a community united; relationships of authentic love. We love our neighbors as our selves, with open hands and by drawing the circle wider to encompass and embrace them. We love our loved-ones as they wish to be loved. The spaces we create together, whether in community or in our intimate relationships, are so safe and so sacred they can hold all our fears along with all our joys. Here, our broken hearts are mended as they are loyally treated as sacrosanct. This is where our allegiance abides, knowing the road to peace is the way of peace and the path to prayer is the path of prayer. We covenant with each other and with God as we merge our hearts with our callings.

Yes, *Living Life as a Prayer*, we embark upon the journey of building The Beloved Community that heals the loneliness that exists in the world. We get through stresses, and even the daunting uncertainties, that occur in our lives: moment by moment. We love humanities children with our whole hearts. In doing so, we create authentic communities within our neighborhoods where all adults are looking out for the best interest of each other's children. Communities that have measures in place to alert residents when dangers exist and systems to protect children therein. We inculcate our children with love and grace, and with patience and gentleness. We provide them with the means to explore the world around them, and attune to Nature.

We build into our *Wheel of the Year* dedicated times of rest, of renewal, of being in intentional isolation with only those we hold most dear. In *Living Life as a Prayer*, Sabbatical Lifestyles are treated as necessary to our wellbeing, and the wellbeing of everyone, equally. We create family and community cultures that are in alignment with our spiritual truths. Including honoring and observing Holy Days.

We acknowledge that grief is part of life's journey. When someone we love dies, we are to give ourselves permission to grieve in the ways that feel right for us. Then we are to give ourselves permission to move forward, knowing this grief will be part of our lives, even as joy for new and beautiful things will be. Grief and joy can and do coexist. We *Live Life as a Prayer* when we accept this and allow it to be so in our lives. Caring for our grief. Welcoming our joy.

Living Life as a Prayer, we cherish the land we reside on. We grow our food, whenever possible, and we bless our land in meaningful ways. Immersing in the water, exploring the woods and forests, walking gently and encouraging others to do the same.

Living Life as a Prayer is living our lives in reverence of Awe and Grace, remembering that, as Rev. Kate Braestrup says,

"*A miracle is not defined by an event. A miracle is defined by gratitude.*"

When we *Live Life as a Prayer,* we are grateful for miracles, magnificent and mundane, and seek to recognize each as they happen.

We give back in ways we can to the people and communities we are part of.

We, thoughtfully, lovingly, share the principles of *Living Life as a Prayer* with others.

We intentionally connect throughout our days with that we which personally identify as Holy, as Sacred.

We remember we are blessed, *we are blessings*, and we bless others as we live our lives as a prayer.

May it be so.

Amen.

Works Cited

Addison Allen, Sarah. *First Frost*. St. Martin's Press. 2015. Print.

Albom, Mitch. *Have a Little Faith*. Sphere Publishing. 2009. Print.

Angels, The City of. Warner Bros. Pictures. 1998. Video.

Aristotle. Greek Philosopher. (384 BC-322 BC). 2014. Web.

Backman, Fredrik. *A Man Called Ove*. 2012. Print.

Barrett, Deborah Ph.D. "The Healing Powers of Sex." *Psychology Today*. 2011. Web.

"Benediction." First Parish in Concord. 2009. Web.

Bentorah, Chaim. "Hebrew Word Study: Revealing The Heart Of God." 2016. Web.

Bogard, Daniel. Facebook. July 28th, 2017. Web.

Brach, Tara. "The Healing Power of Self-Compassion" (Part 2) 2011. Web.

Braden, Gregg. *Secrets of the Lost Mode of Prayer: The Hidden Power of Beauty, Blessing, Wisdom, and Hurt*. Hay House. 2006. Print.

Bradstreet, Anne. "Contemplations." Written 1679. Poetry Foundation. 2015. Web.

Braestrup, Kate. *Here if You Need Me*. Little, Brown and Company. 2007. Print.

Brown, Brené. *The Anatomy of Trust*. Super Soul Sessions. 2015. Web.

Bush, Dr. Zach. Facebook. 2020. Web.

Cameron, Julia. *The Artist's Way for Parents.* Penguin Group. 2013. Print.

Castaneda, Carlos. *The Active Side of Infinity.* Harper Collins Publishers. 1999. Print

Chapman, Gary. *The Five Love Languages: How to Express Heartfelt Commitment to Your Mate.* 1995. Print.

Childre, Doc Lew. *Freeze-frame.* HeartMath LLC. 1998. Print.

Coelho, Paulo. *The Witch of Portobello.* (p 65) Harper Collins. 2007. Print.

Cole, Nat King. "Nature Boy." Capitol Records. 1948. Audio.

Darnell, John Coleman. *Elkab Desert Archaeological Survey Project.* 2017. Web.

Day, Laura. *The Circle: How the Power of a Single Wish Can Change Your Life.* Atria Books. 2009. Print.

Corn, Seane. *Revolution of the Soul.* Sounds True Incorporated. 2019. Print and "Your Pain is your Purpose" video.

Crow, Sheryl. "Love Will Remain." 2010. Audio.

"Desire." *Online Etymology Dictionary.* 2017. Web.

Drydakis, Nick. *The Journal of Gerontology. Women's Health Magazine.* 2014. Web.

Druidic Craft of the Wise: Student Handbook. Grove of the Sacred Oak Press. 2005. Print.

Dylan, Bob. "All Along The Watchtower." 1967. Audio.

Dunne, Finley Peter. "Mr. Dooley on Newspaper Publicity." 1902. Web.

Eckhart, Meister. 13th Century. ((see below: Stivers, Cathie)).

Emerson, Ralph Waldo. "Friendship," "Always Something Sings," "Over-Soul." *2014*. Web.

Fromm, Erich. *The Art of Loving*. Harper. 1956. Print.

Gibran, Khalil. "Love One Another." 2013. Web.

Goldberg, Natalie. *Writing Down the Bones, Freeing the Writer Within*. Shambhala. 2005. Print.

Hanh, Thich Nhat. *True Love: A Practice for Awakening the Heart*. Shambhala. 2006. Print.

Hill, Julia Butterfly.

Horton-Ludwig, Rev. Laura. "Sexuality and Spirituality." *Sermon*. 2016. Video.

Humphries, Pat. "Swimming to the Other Side." 2001. Audio.

Irish Blessing for Hospitality. Edward Hayes Website. 2016. Web

Jobim, Antonio Carlos. "Wave." A&M Records. 1967. Audio.

Jones, Sarah Dan. "When I Breathe In." 2005. Web. (alternate full original song version: https://youtu.be/Ye-oRQoQarc)

Jung, Carl. *Psychology and Religion*. Yale University Press. 1960. Print

King, Jr, Martin Luther. *Birth of A New Nation, 1957*. The King Center. 2015. Web.

King, Rev. Naomi. Blog. 2014. Web.

"Kintsugi." *Wikipedia*. 2017. Web.

Krznaric, Roman. "The Ancient Greeks' 6 Words for Love (And Why Knowing Them Can Change Your Life)." *Yes! Magazine*. 2013. Web.

Lamott, Anne. *Bird by Bird: Some Instructions on Writing and Life*. Anchor. 1995. Print

---. *Small Victories: Spotting Improbable Moments of Grace*. 2014. Print.

Lane Jr., Phil, Hereditary Chief. ((see below: Stivers, Cathie)).

Lavanhar, Rev. Marlin. Sermon: "Why Life is Not Fair." 2013. Video

Lemelson, Robert. Article: "In Bali, Babies Are Believed Too Holy to Touch the Earth." *New York Times*. 2017. Web.

Lennon, John. "Imagine." Apple Records. 1971. Audio.

Lindbergh, Anne Morrow. *Gift from the Sea*. Pantheon Books. 1955. Print.

Maher, Rev. Ian White. "Prophetic Evangelism." *Podcast*. 2017. Audio.

Markham, Edwin. "Outwitted." 2017. Web.

Martineau, James. *A Martineau Year Book: Extracts of Sermons*. Forgotten Books Press. 2015. Print

Masters, Dr. Paul Leon. "Loneliness - Mystically Perceived." *Mystical Insights Newsletter*. November 22, 2015. Email.

Mercola, Dr.. *The Top 11 Benefits of Sex*. Mercola.com. 2013. Web.

McDade and Schuck Longview, Carolyn and Lucile. "Coming Home, Like Rivers to the Sea: A Woman's Ritual."

McInerny, Nora. *"We Don't 'Move on' from Grief. We Move Forward with It."* TEDWomen. 2018. Video.

Miller, Mona. *Invisible Warfare.* Communication Arts Company. 2007. Print

Montgomery, Lucy Maude. *Anne of Green Gables.* 1908. Print.

Moore, Thomas. *The Soul of Sex: Cultivating Life as an Act of Love* HarperPerennial. 1998. Print.

Morales, Peter. "Service is Our Prayer." UU World. 2010. Web.

Morgan, Angela. "Kinship." 1936. Print.

Niebuhr, Reinhold. "The Serenity Prayer." 1932-33. Web.

O'Donohue, John. *Anam Ċara: A Book of Celtic Wisdom.* Harper Perennial. 1998. Print.

Oliver, Mary. Poem: "The Summer Day." *House of Light.* Beacon Press. 1990. Print.

Oppenheimer, Sharifa. *Heaven on Earth: a Handbook for Parents of Young Children.* SteinerBooks. 2006. Print.

Phyllis, Carl. *PEI Potters Guild.* circa 1997. In Person.

"Raku." *Merriam Webster Dictionary.* 2017. Web.

Reese Lett, Rev. Dr. Della. *Metaphysically Speaking: The Bible is the Greatest How-To Book Ever Written.* Lett/Reese International Publishing. 2012. Print.

Richards, M.C.. *Centering: in Pottery, Poetry, and the Person.* Wesleyan University Press. 1964. Print.

Riley, Rev. Meg. 2016. Web.

Roberts, Jane. *The Seth Learning Center.* 2016. Web.

Roberts, Nora. *Charmed*. (prologue) Silhouette. 1992. Print.

Royce, Josiah. "1915 Fellowship of Reconciliation." *Stanford Encyclopedia of Philosophy*. 2014. Web.

Ruffin, Rev. David. "Transcending Together." *Sermon*. 2015. Video.

Rūmī, Jalāl ad-Dīn Muhammad. 13th Century.

Saint Francis of Assisi. (1181/82-1226).

Sarton, May. *Catching Beauty*. Puckerbrush Press. 2002. Print

Schucman, Helen. *A Course in Miracles*. Miracles Center Website. 1976. Web.

Scott King, Coretta. ""The Greatness of a Community." 2000. Web.

Shick, Stephen. "This Sacred Place." *Skinner House*. 2009. Print.

Sharma, Robin. *The Monk Who Sold His Ferrari*. Harper One. 1997. Print.

Shuttee, Patricia. "The Winds of Summer." 1992. Web.

Simard, Suzanne. Toomey, Diane. "Exploring How and Why Trees 'Talk' to Each Other." 2016. Web.

Smith Koehler, Linda. *Women With Wings: Original Chants and Songs of Affirmation and Empowerment*. Quiet Waters Publications, 2005. Print.

Solomon, Art. "Ojibway Prayer." World Council of Churches Meeting. 1983. Web.

Starhawk. *Dreaming the Dark: Magic, Sex and Politics*. Beacon Press. 1998. Print.

Stivers, Cathie. *Reviving Our Indigenous Souls, How to Practice the Ancient to Bring in the New.* BalboaPress. 2018. Print.

The Holy Bible. New International Version. Bible Gateway. Web.
---. Deuteronomy 25:17,18
---. 1 Samuel 15:18
---. Psalm 14:1
---. Book of Ecclesiastes
---. Matthew 6:24
---. Matthew 7:12
---. Matthew 12:31
---. 1 Corinthians 13:11-14
---. Isaiah 58

Thoreau, Henry David. *Walden.* Bantam Books. 1962. Print.

Tolle, Eckhart. *Stillness Speaks.* Namaste Publishing. 2003. Print.

Tsabary, Dr. Shefali. Super Soul Sessions. OWN. 2016, 2020. Video.

Velie, Dianalee. "Laughter." *First Edition.* Rock Village Publishing. 2005. Print.

Wallace, David Foster. "This is Water." *Commencement Speech.* 2005. Audio.

Whyte, David. *Excerpts from Consolations: The Solace, Nourishment and Underlying Meaning of Everyday Words.* Many Rivers Press. 2014. Web.

#LivingLifeAsAPrayer #PiecesOfPeaceOnEarth #PulpitOfPeace
#TheChurchOfKineo #Rsotde #MooseheadLakeReatreats
#MooseheadLakeWeddings #TwinklesPlace

Acknowledgements

The citations on the previous pages list some of the most influential spiritual leaders, authors, poets and musicians who have touched my life and informed my spirituality. There are quite literally a hundred more I could add that inspire me, plus dozens of family and friends who have been my biggest supporters. For the sake of brevity, *(inasmuch as I can ever accomplish anything close to brevity)* I will say this:

My life is blessed by the love of my husband, Ed Porter. He encourages me to do the work I am called to. He has helped make many dreams come true, including encouraging me to establish *The Church of Kineo*. Our home, our blended family, our children and grandchildren - sharing these with him makes my heart sing every single day.

My life is blessed with our children: Dylan, Morgan, Riley, Orion, Cameron, Karissa, Josie. And, our grandchildren: Kai, Zoey, Gabe, Cayson, Lila, River.

My life is blessed by the love and connection with my siblings and their partners: Audrey & Paul, Charlie, Laura & Steve, Steafan & Tim. And relatives I count as siblings: Gary, Lynn, Mignon. Paul Beaton. And, my nieces and nephews: Paul (PJ), Owen, Grace, Asa; Daniel, Arressa Marie; Autumn, Willa. And relatives I count as nieces and nephews: Ben, Becca. Sam, Alex.

My life is blessed by my mother-in-law, Sandra Porter. My former parents-in-law: Eunice & Doug Brenton. By Diane & JT Curran. And, of course, my own parents who transitioned from this world far too early.

My life is blessed with sister-like friendships that help keep me whole through celebration in joyful times, witness in sorrow-filled times, and with mutual respect and abiding love: Carmen Lohn, Holly Rose, Jo Riddell, Lorraine Martin, Starr Ratcliff, Sandra Coles, Karen McAlpine Orlando.

My life is blessed with friends who support me and love me and affirm me regardless of distances in time and geography: Vicki Hyde Gillis, Colleen Gallant Williams, Bernadette Rombough. Bozena Smith, Margaret Stewart, Suzanne Foley. Carmela Thompson. Suu Feathers, Anca van Assendelft, Joan Amaral. Barry Parsons. Gary Broughman. Jeff Coyne.

My life is blessed with new families of friends who have welcomed me with open arms in Maine: Shannon & Darrell Spaulding, Tammy & Steve George, Trudy & Lance Richmond, Kristin Gagnon, Kellie Duplisea, Andrea & Aaron McCannell, Darcy & Ronny Rollins, Carrie & Mark Mancini, and Heather & Wayne Sinclair.

My life is blessed with colleagues who are mentors and friends who light the way through the dark moments of the soul, creating space sacred-enough for the rawest of emotions and welcoming-enough for joy to find its way through the thresholds of grief: Rev. Bonnie Tarwater, Rev. Ian White Maher, Rev. Maddie Sifantus and Rev. Jess Tardy you have saved my spirit and renewed my faith over and over and over.

My life is blessed with seers and believers who through their work bring magic into the world: Kris Oster, Katherine Glass, Cheryl Partridge, Carolena Presto and Mary Cuchetti Roig, thank you.

My life is blessed.

Amen.

Holy Days: The Church of Kineo

The Church of Kineo recognizes the liturgical seasons of neighboring faiths and is especially attuned to honoring the Christian, Pagan, and Esoteric calendars of holy days by observation, participation and facilitation of interfaith services. Within our own tradition, we honor the cycles and seasons of the Earth, as well as the cycles and seasons of our bodies, marking milestones and thresholds with ritual.

We also have our own designated sacred Holy Days, including Sundays and Mondays (for clergy) as our weekly Sabbath Days. We believe in living a Sabbatical Lifestyle and as we grow we will add more Holy Days as in alignment with the principles of *Living Life as a Prayer*.

As an example, these are some of the days we observe as sacred each year:

January 1st - New Year's Day
June 15th - Founder's Day
July 13th - Sacred Couples Day
September 1st - October 5th - Our Holy Month*
September 16th-20th Deep Reflection Days*
October 13th - Promise Day
October 31st - Sacred Darkness Day
November 8th - Soul Friend's Day
December 20th - Light of the World Day
December 24th - Christmas Eve
December 25th - Christmas Day
December 26th - Boxing Day

* *among our High Holy Days*

Additional holidays include Mother's Day, Father's Day, Thanksgiving Day, and the Month of November our *Gratitude Month*. For up to date information and more details about each of our Holy Days, visit: www.TheChurchOfKineo.org

REFLECTIONS

What additional discernments are coming through to you as you explore the principles of Living Life as a Prayer? Use these pages to write and draw your inspirations, thoughts and feelings.

BLESSING BOOK SERIES

Uniquely designed to be journals, spiritual exploration tools and self-led retreats, *Blessing Books* can be used to mark a milestone such as a significant birthday or important season of your life. *Blessing Books* can help you process a loss or transition. It can be where you express your gratitude or your grief. It can be the place you affirm what is next for you as you cross a threshold and visualize your greatest intention for your life. Essentially, *Blessing Books* are where you can contemplate and document your inner-most thoughts, feelings, beliefs and experiences.

Wherever you are on your journey, and in both times of joy and in times of sorrow, may these books serve you well.

For additional *Blessing Book* themes and meditation tools, visit:

www.MatrikaPress.com/blessing-books

www.MatrikaPress.com/30-days-of-reflection

www.MatrikaPress.com/family-blessing-book

www.MatrikaPress.com/blue-christmas

www.MatrikaPress.com/moosehead-lake-reflections

www.MatrikaPress.com/blessing-books

Women's Virtual Minerva Potlucks

*Minerva is the Goddess of Wisdom and Poetry. We will share both, and more, at these gatherings.

JOIN US ONLINE via ZOOM!
www.TheChurchOfKineo.org/
WomensSpirituality

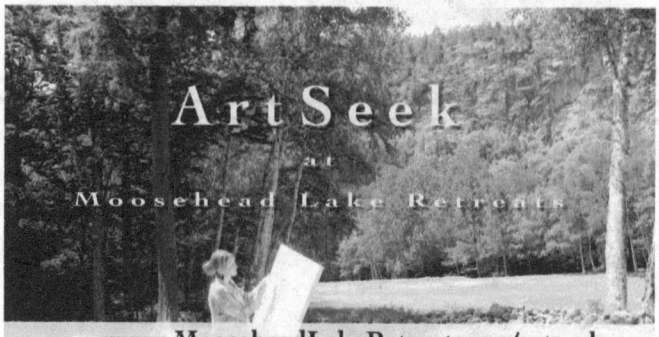

Moosehead Lake Retreats
offers a variety of packages as well as customized retreats and workshops designed to meet your needs and mindfully nurture your body, mind and spirit.
Join Us!

Moosehead Lake area offers beautiful Lakeside, Woods and Beach locations. Where ever on or near Moosehead Lake your wedding is taking place, be it a large or small gathering, luxurious or rustic, Rev. Manning's wedding officiant services can be customized to create your dream-come-true wedding ceremony.

About the Author

Rev. "Twinkle" Marie Porter-Manning is the senior minister of The Church of Kineo, an emerging ministry founded in the principles of *Living Life as a Prayer*. She is an interfaith minister, wedding officiant, skilled ritualist and liturgist who has been leading workshops and seminars in the secular and spiritual worlds for more than two decades. She actively develops and leads programs that nourish spirituality. Her rituals, reflections and poetry have been included internationally in all manner of worship services and publications.

Rev. Manning's community ministry has long been known affectionately as Twinkle's Place, where she hosts a variety of retreats and spiritual programs. Her work as a television producer with TV for Your Soul has created many series of programs that enrich people's lives. She has authored several books, including *Women of Spirit, Exploring Sacred Paths of Wisdom Keepers, Intentional Visualization*, and the *Blessing Book series*.

As an artist and a writer, she finds great inspiration in the natural world, and the magic seen and unseen therein. She shares a home in Rockwood, Maine with her husband. Their blended family includes three daughters, four sons, and six grandchildren.

www.MatrikaPress.com/twinkle-marie-manning
www.TheChurchOfKineo.org
www.MooseheadLakeWeddings.org
www.MooseheadLakeRetreats.org
www.TwinklesPlace.org

Living Life as a Prayer

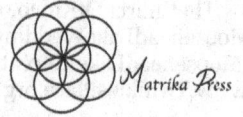

www.ingramcontent.com/pod-product-compliance
Lightning Source LLC
Chambersburg PA
CBHW010741290426
43661CB00091BB/958